D0567766

SET MY SPIRIT FREE

Set My Spirit Free

DR. ROBERT C. FROST

LOGOS INTERNATIONAL/*Plainfield, New Jersey*

*Scripture quotations are from the King James version
unless otherwise identified.*

SET MY SPIRIT FREE

© 1973 by Logos, International
Plainfield, New Jersey 07060
Printed in the United States of America
Library of Congress Catalog Card Number: 73-84475
ISBN: 0-88270-057-x (hardcover)
       0-88270-058-8 (softcover)

We wish to acknowledge the use of the following copyrighted publications; quotations from them are identified by symbols in parentheses.

(TAB) THE AMPLIFIED BIBLE (Grand Rapids, Mich.: Zondervan, 1965).

(Phillips) THE NEW TESTAMENT IN MODERN ENG-LISH, tr. by J. B. Phillips (New York, N.Y.: Macmillan, 1958).

(TLB) THE LIVING BIBLE (Wheaton, Ill.: Tyndale House, 1971).

(NAB) NEW AMERICAN BIBLE (Washington, D.C.: Catholic Book Publishing Company, 1970).

(NASB) NEW AMERICAN STANDARD BIBLE (Carol Stream, Ill.: Creation House, 1971).

(RSV) THE HOLY BIBLE: REVISED STANDARD VERSION (New York, N.Y.: Thomas Nelson & Sons, 1952).

(NEB) THE NEW ENGLISH BIBLE (New York, N.Y.: Oxford Univ. Press, 1961).

PREFACE

The Body of Christ will be only as strong and healthy as its members. Each part of the Body has a place and a purpose. Proper alignment and full functioning of each individual member is essential if the church of Jesus Christ is to present to the world a powerful and living testimony of God's love, joy, and peace. It is this glorious gospel of the Kingdom in the midst of hate, sorrow, and turmoil which will provide men with a confrontation with our Living Lord. This is the end-time, worldwide witness which Jesus promised would usher in His Second Coming (Matt. 24:3,14).

For this reason, there has been an unusual emphasis by the Holy Spirit upon restoring God's people to a place of spiritual health and vitality. The Lord Himself is releasing them from inner hurts and pain from past experiences of all types. Spiritual cripples are being healed and walking forth in resurrection power to share their newfound freedom with others. The sons and daughters of the King are arising from their beds of affliction and moving out as a mighty army, steady in faith, and strong in the truth. There is no doubt about it—God is preparing His people for the return of His Son and their Redeemer.

The purpose of this book is to acquaint the reader with the role God has given His Spirit in the liberation of our lives. Only as we ourselves have been healed within can we help a world without which is hurt and needs God's healing power.

We need to know what we have in Holy Spirit Baptism—and what has us—if we are to walk consistently in truth and liberty.

Our approach will involve a study of a number of descriptive phrases found in the Bible which relate to our life in the Spirit. The terms are used interchangeably throughout the Scriptures, but each has a particular emphasis which is necessary for a balanced walk with God. We limp and wobble along sometimes because we are still crippled within, and need the healing power of the Holy Spirit to touch us where we hurt.

Our presentation will be primarily descriptive and experiential, rather than doctrinal or theological. The various phrases to be considered are listed in the chapter headings. Each speaks uniquely to some practical area of need in our personal lives, and relates that need to the answer which is found in Christ Jesus. "If the Son therefore shall make you free, ye shall be free indeed (actually, truly really)."

As the Holy Spirit reveals to us the Lordship of Jesus, the hold of the Adversary on our lives is broken. God's Word has been repeatedly proven in practice. It is truly life-releasing! Many of the illustrations described in the following pages are actual experiences of people who have been set free by the releasing power of God's Holy Spirit.

It is the prayer and expectation of the author that the Lord will honor the written word in the life of each reader, as He has already honored that same word in its spoken form. This can be your hour for inner healing. Let us join together even now and make this expectation a confession in faith.

CONTENTS

SET MY SPIRIT FREE

1

THE PROMISE
OF THE FATHER

A Sure Word

Fear not, O land; be glad and rejoice: for the Lord will do great things. . . . And ye shall know I am in the midst of Israel, and that I am the Lord your God, and none else: and my people shall never be ashamed. And it shall come to pass afterward, that I will pour out my spirit upon all flesh . . . And also upon the servants and upon the handmaids in those days will I pour out my spirit. (Joel 2:21, 27–29)

If ye then, being evil, know how to give good gifts unto your children: how much more shall your heavenly *Father* give the Holy Spirit to them that ask him? (Luke 11:13)

I will pray the *Father,* and he shall give you another Comforter, that he may abide with you for ever. (John 14:16)

But the comforter, which is the Holy Ghost, whom the *Father* will send in my name, he shall teach you all things. (John 14:26)

But when the Comforter is come, whom I will send unto you from the *Father,* even the Spirit of truth, which proceedeth from the *Father,* he shall testify of me. (John 15:26)

And, behold, I send the *promise of my Father* upon you: but tarry ye in the city of Jerusalem, until ye be endued with power from on high. (Luke 24:49)

1

And, being assembled together with them, [Jesus] commanded them that they should not depart from Jerusalem, but wait for the *promise of the Father,* which, saith he, ye have heard of me. (Acts 1:4)

And when the day of Pentecost was fully come . . . they were all filled with the Holy Ghost, and began to speak with other tongues, as the Spirit gave them utterance. (Acts 2:1,4)

Therefore being by the right hand of God exalted, and having received *of the Father the promise of the Holy Ghost* . . . [Jesus] shed forth this, which ye now see and hear. (Acts 2:33)

The *promise* is unto you, and to your children, and to all that are afar off. (Acts 2:39)

After that ye believed, ye were sealed with that *holy Spirit of promise.* (Eph. 1:13)

Christ hath redeemed us from the curse of the law . . . That the blessing of Abraham might come on the Gentiles through Jesus Christ; that we might receive the *promise of the Spirit* through faith. (Gal. 3:13–14)

The "promise of the Father" is a theme which can be traced through Scripture. It begins with the prophets of the Old Testament and is personally re-emphasized by Jesus in the Gospels. The fulfillment of the promise for the disciples and early New Testament believers is found in the Book of Acts. The appropriation and application of the promise is carefully interpreted throughout the Epistles.

Words and phrases often have the ability to stimulate the inner senses of the soul. They can be colorful or drab, fragrant or foul, warm or cold, soft or sharp, pleasant or painful, full of flavor or insipid, peaceful or perturbing—depending upon the intention of the author. The Holy Spirit through the authorship of inspired men speaks to us from the understanding and affections of our Heavenly Father. It is necessary for us, therefore, to listen not only with our heads, but also with our hearts—to think and to feel. An enlightened mind may set a new direction for life, but it is often the heart which provides the motive power.

THE FATHERHOOD OF GOD

The phrase, "promise of the Father," has always produced a warm feeling within my heart. There is something about the fatherhood of God which conveys a sense of loving care and concern. My own father died when I was three. In my teenage years, the little expression, "my son," so frequently used in the Book of Proverbs, helped provide the paternal counsel I wanted and needed. Now that I have my own family, I appreciate more than ever the fatherliness of God. Sonship and daughterhood in God's family is a very special relationship.

Many times in praying with people I have sensed the love of the Father for His children. Frequently the Spirit assures those who are hesitant and feel unworthy in their own sight, that they are beloved sons and daughters in the family of their Heavenly Father. Just to be loved of God creates a sense of personal worthwhileness. The Father so loved you and me that He exhausted the very treasury of heaven in sending His Son to die for our sins that we might enjoy living together in His family forever. Love confers the worthiness of the giver upon the recipient.

Many whose earthly fathers were cruel or unloving find it difficult to picture their Heavenly Father with anything but a frown, evoking cold, distant, and even fearful feelings. They can more readily respond with affection to the love of Jesus. Actually, Jesus tried to relate His disciples more intimately with the Father when He plainly told them that anyone who had seen Him (Jesus) had seen the Father (John 14:9). Jesus fully and personally expressed the love of the Father in the universal language of everyday life.

I remember a young teenage girl, crying for joy after the Holy Spirit had revealed her Heavenly Father to her through the love of Jesus. A hurt in her life regarding her earthly father had been healed, and she was released from a bondage of years' standing. She confessed through tears that it was the first time in her life she knew what the love of a father was really like! To find Jesus is to find the Father; to know Jesus is to know the Father; to love Jesus is to love the Father; for Jesus said, "I and the Father are one" (John 10:30).

The Psalms reflect the warmth and understanding with which David recognized the fatherhood of God:

> As a father pities his children, so the Lord pities them that fear (reverence) Him. For He knows our frame (fashioned from clay) and earnestly remembers that we are dust. (Ps. 103:13–14 various versions)

The word "pity," *racham* in Hebrew, means, literally, "to fondle," and conveys the feeling of love and compassion for little children. Jesus, in His desire to reveal the affection of His Father, gathered the little children around Him and blessed them. One Gospel record says, "He took the children up one by one in His arms, put His hands upon them, and lovingly blessed them" (Mark 10:16 various versions).

The same feeling carries over into other New Testament passages:

> Blessed [be] the God and Father of our Lord Jesus Christ, the Father of sympathy (pity and mercies) and the God . . . of every consolation and comfort and encouragement. (II Cor. 1:3 TAB)

> So be merciful—sympathetic, tender, responsive and compassionate—even as your Father is. (Luke 6:36 TAB)

> The Lord is very *pitiful,* and of tender mercy. (James 5:11)

The Greek term for "pitiful" (*polusplanchnos*), as found in the passage above, means literally, "much heart" or "extremely affectionate and compassionate." It would appear that the Holy Spirit has most emphatically sought to convey to us through God's Word that our Heavenly Father does indeed care for us and loves each one of us very much. (Calvary love was most desperate in its expression.)

John, the Beloved Disciple, summarizes the whole theme in one of his epistles:

> See what an incredible quality of love the Father has given us, that we should be named and called and counted the children of God! And so we are! . . . Beloved, we are here and now God's children; it is not yet clear what we shall be hereafter, but we know that when He comes we shall, as God's children, be like Him, for we shall see Him just as He really is. (I john 3:1–2 TAB, modified)

The Hidden Desire of the Father's Heart

Our Heavenly Father has had hidden in His heart from even before the foundation of the world a glorious plan, glorious because it is centered in the glorious person—of His Son. Glimpses were caught by the prophets of the Old Testament, although much of the mystery was hidden in the types and shadows of Israelite worship and ceremonial law. When the fullness of time arrived, God's Son was sent to this world to fulfill the will of the Father.

The plan had actually been initiated with the creation of Adam. Tragedy befell the first family, however, and for a time, it seemed as if the serpent had thwarted the eternal purpose of God. But inherent within the divine plan was a redemptive function. Where the first Adam had failed, through the redemptive work of Jesus, the Second Adam, God's original desire would be fulfilled.

Little was known concerning the magnitude of the Father's will while Jesus was here on earth. He endeavored to prepare the people, and especially His disciples, by teaching them concerning the Kingdom of God. The heavenly, spiritual quality of the Kingdom was quite foreign to them, and they persisted in their efforts to reduce the concept to an earthly level. Their minds were veiled, and it was difficult for them to visualize anything else.

The Lord finally crushed this earthly concept of the Kingdom, but it involved the crucifixion of their King! A whole new horizon developed, however, upon His resurrection. A seed had been sown, and soon there was to be a harvest. The Father's will on earth was going to be done. The eternal plan was coming into focus and fulfillment. The day of promise had arrived.

It took a trip to the third heaven by the apostle Paul to bring all of the details of the divine plan into sharp relief. He was given the unusual opportunity of looking back through the ages into the eternal counsel and fellowship of the Godhead. The Father allowed Paul to place his hands upon the pulsating desire which had been hidden so long deep in His heart. What he saw and what he felt, changed his entire life—as it will ours, if we can see and feel what he did.

What was this magnificent plan? Listen to the words of the apostle Paul himself:

Long ago, even before he made the world, God chose us to be his very own, through what Christ would do for us; he decided then to make us holy in his eyes, without a single fault—we who stand before him covered with his love. His unchanging plan has always been to adopt us into his own family by sending Jesus Christ to die for us. And he did this because he wanted to! (Eph. 1:4–5 TLB)

God has told us his secret reason for sending Christ, a plan he decided on in mercy long ago; and this was his purpose: that when the time is ripe he will gather us all together from wherever we are—in heaven or on earth—to be with him in Christ, forever. (Eph. 1:9–10 TLB)

For from the very beginning God decided that those who came to him—and all along he knew who would—should become like his Son, so that his Son would be the First, with many brothers. And having chosen us, he called us to come to him; and when we came, he declared us "not guilty," filled us with Christ's goodness, gave us right standing with himself, and promised us his glory. What can we ever say to such wonderful things as these? If God is on our side, who can ever be against us? (Rom. 8:29–31 TLB)

The warm loving relationship which the Father has enjoyed with the Son from all eternity is to be extended to include an everlasting family of many sons and daughters. The members of this family are to inherit and express the life and nature of their Elder and Model Brother, the Lord Jesus Christ. Only in Him does the Father find true pleasure and delight.

This family relationship is not an automatic privilege, but one which is ours by right of birth—a new birth. Jesus informed Nicodemus, a religious leader among the Jews, that he needed to be "born again." Just as the avenue into an earthly family is the process of natural birth, so the avenue into the family of our Heavenly Father is a spiritual birth.

An impartation of life is necessary in both cases. In regard to our heavenly family relationship, that impartation is a person—the Lord Jesus Christ. He is our life everlasting (John 14:6; I John 5:12). To receive Him as Lord and Savior is to receive eternal life, and find our place in the Father's family—forever (John 1:12).

There is a quality to this divine life which is ever fresh and increasingly beautiful. God has created each one of us to be unique, and we can find ourselves as persons only as we find ourselves in God's family through the redeeming grace of Jesus. There is no other way to tie into divine and eternal purpose. God planned it so.

To be born into the family of God is to discover we have inherited a new name (God's), a new nature (God's), and a whole host of brothers and sisters. Our Lord and Savior becomes our Elder and Model Brother, in whose image man was originally created. For the first time, we can truly call God our Heavenly Father. Only through Jesus can we find real sonship with God (John 14:6).

THE SIGNIFICANCE OF SONSHIP

Sonship involves a dual relationship of intimacy and respect. The apostle Paul not only grasped the full meaning of this with his mind, but he felt something in his heart which was deeply moving:

> For all who are led by the Spirit of God are sons of God. And so we should not be like cringing, fearful slaves, but we should behave like God's very own children, adopted into the bosom of his family, and calling to him, "Father, Father." For his Holy Spirit speaks to us deep in our hearts, and tells us that we really are God's children. And since we are his children, we shall share his treasures—for all God gives to his Son Jesus is now ours too. (Rom. 8:14–17 TLB)

The word "Father" (*Abba*) in the above passage has a beautiful and most personal meaning. Jesus used the term while praying to His Father in the Garden of Gethsemane (Mark 14:36). Paul uses the term again in his Epistle to the Galatians where the context is quite similar to the passage in Romans:

> And because you really are His sons, God has sent the Holy Spirit of His Son into our hearts, crying, "Abba, Father!" (Gal. 4:6 TAB, modified)

"Abba" is an ramaic expre sion of intimate endearment. It was probably one of the first words which a little child learned to speak, similar in English to "Daddy" or "Papa." It conveyed a childlike, unreasoning trust based simply on love. The word "Father" involved a more intelligent, mature appreciation of the family relationship. The two terms together, "Abba, Father," linked the feeling and thoughtful insight which the concept of divine fatherhood conveys to a trusting child of God.

The combination of terms is sometimes translated, "my Father" or "dear Father." I suppose one could translate the terms as "Papa, Father" or "Daddy, Father" as well. There is something of the little boy and little girl that remains within all of us, regardless of age. Often in times of crisis or distress, feelings from childhood days flood our lives as we sense our need for security, love, and understanding. In any case, the intimate feeling of personal endearment coupled with profound respect is well appreciated by the child of God whose Spirit has been set free by the Truth.

As the Son of Man, Jesus experienced the full range of human feelings, yet without weakness or compromise. As a young child, Jesus received the first impressions of what His Heavenly Father was like from the life, words, and face of Joseph.

How often He had felt the strong, reassuring arms of Joseph around Him during childhood times of sadness and disappointment. It was Joseph's tender touch which comforted the little boy whose finger was cut in the carpenter shop. It was to him He went for fatherly counsel and wisdom when perplexing affairs bewildered a young lad who was learning the ways of this world. Joseph, I am sure, was always careful to relate the boy, Jesus, to His Heavenly Father as He matured, and godly responsibility and dependence were divinely developed. Upon the death of Joseph, the transfer from the earthly relationship to the heavenly was complete. Joseph had fulfilled his God-given responsibility well.

As the Lord faced the reality of the cross before Him, His agony of soul became intense. He had never known what broken fellowship from the Father would be like, but now it was only hours away. He who knew no sin was going to become sin (yours and mine) and actually experience the horror of spiritual death—separation from His Heavenly Father (II Cor. 5:21; Rom. 6:23).

With great intensity of feeling He cried out, "Abba, Father, all things are possible unto thee; take away this cup from me: nevertheless not what I will, but what thou wilt" (Mark 14:36). The relationship of love, faith, and obedience between the Father and the Son found their finest expression in this hour. The Son turned to His Father in this moment of terrifying anticipation and accepted assurance of His presence. He then resolutely submited to His will, confident that the Father's love would ultimately triumph over sin, Satan, and the grave. "Abba, Father" took on its full meaning—it was the confession of a Son to His Father from a heart filled with faith, hope, and love.

The Holy Spirit wants us to be free to receive our Father's love and to express our love to Him. Perhaps it would be appropriate at this point to address our Father God in prayer:

Father, my Father, my dear Heavenly Father! In childlike simplicity, I accept Your love for me, and I want You to accept my love and appreciation for You. Thank You for Your Son, for through Him I have discovered You and found my place in Your family. I now join my voice with those of my brothers and sisters everywhere, and together from the depths of our hearts to Yours we cry out, "Abba, Father!"

THE PROMISE: ITS PURPOSE AND POWER

Yes, we have a wonderful Heavenly Father, and He has given us a wonderful promise. It is the promise of His Spirit, which is to forever fill our lives to overflowing. Furthermore, there is a purpose behind the promise, for God's will can never be fulfilled apart from the power of His Spirit. He knows our frame was fashioned from clay, and that the might and power of men even at their best can never accomplish His glorious will for their lives (Zech. 4:6).

God's purpose for His children is that they find their place and function in His family. Each person has a divine call and unique ministry for his life which only the Holy Spirit can fulfill. Purpose without power can be frustrating, but our Father has made provision for both. Our destiny is to find ourselves in Jesus, and He really is the only place our self-discovery can be made! As we find ourselves in Him, we shall increasingly become like Him in our thoughts, words, and deeds, yet in the unique way that God created us as individuals. It is a rather strange paradox, but we become ourselves as we deny ourselves, take up our cross, and follow Him (Matt. 16:24–25).

It takes power, however, to die as well as to live. I can't take up my cross, let alone follow Jesus, without some resource greater than myself. The Father recognizes that need and has promised the power necessary for his handmaidens and menservants to fulfill their calling. The provision is related to a Person, the Holy Spirit, Himself. No wonder Jesus cautioned His disciples to tarry in Jerusalem for the "promise of the Father," for with it was to come an endowment of power.

The need for overcoming power was what drove me to Jesus for His Baptism in the Holy Spirit. I loved the Lord, and knew I was indwelt by His Spirit, but the power of that Spirit needed to be released. I was weak and wobbly, spiritually speaking. I needed to be filled and flooded to overflowing with the power of God's love.

I have come to realize that God has a special love for those who feel they are weak and worthless. We must see this, or the Enemy will use our sense of unworthiness to keep us from coming to the Father in faith. How many times have we not heard (perhaps from our own lips) the little words, "But I don't feel I'm worthy"? They are little words, but they erect big barriers between us and God and His gifts.

The word "promise" (*epangelia*) in the Greek refers to a gift graciously bestowed, not a pledge secured by negotiation. It is a mercy to be received, not a reward to be earned. It is an assurance freely made and freely given. In other words, Holy Spirit Baptism is the promise of a loving Heavenly Father who realizes that His children need divine power in their lives which only He can provide. It is a gift of grace for those who choose to trust and obey (Gal. 3:14; Acts 5:32).

After months of searching, begging, pleading, and self-effort of all sorts, I finally saw the simplicity of coming to my Heavenly Father as a son in childlike faith. He knew my need and desire and had faithfully promised He would endue my life with the power of His Spirit. And it happened—just like He promised. For me it was a mighty Baptism of love that flooded my life inside and out. I could hardly believe it, and kept telling the Lord I wasn't worthy. He informed me that He already knew that, but He loved me anyway. His love wasn't based on my worthiness or faithfulness, but His. I discovered something about the love of our Heavenly Father I had never known before—He loved me exactly as I was.

I also realized that while the Gift was freely given and received, I was now responsible for its possession. The Father promised to take me as I was, that by His Spirit He might make me more and more like His lovely Son. There is a long way to go, but now I have a hope in my heart and a perfecting power in my life. My Heavenly Father had kept His word and performed His promise—and He will do the same for you.

> Stagger not at the promise of God through unbelief; but be strong in faith, giving glory to God; and be fully persuaded that what He has promised, He is also able to perform. (adapted from Rom. 4:20–21)

2

RECEIVING AND RESPONDING

A Gracious Gift

And I say unto you, *Ask* and it shall be *given* you . . . for everyone that *asks, receives.* If a son *ask* his father for bread, would he *give* him a stone? Or for fish, a serpent? Or for an egg, a scorpion? If you who are evil know how to *give* good *gifts* to your children, is not your heavenly Father much more ready to *give* the Holy Spirit to them that *ask* Him? (Luke 11:9–13 various versions)

If any man thirst, let him come unto me and drink. He that believes on me, as the scriptures have said, out of his innermost being shall continually flow rivers of living water. He referred to the Spirit which those who believed in Him were to *receive,* for the Holy Spirit was not yet *given.* (John 7:37–39 various versions)

And He breathed on them and said, *Receive* the Holy Spirit. (John 20:22 various versions)

Then Peter said, Repent and be baptized . . . and you shall *receive* the *gift* of the Holy Spirit. (Acts 2:38 various versions)

And we are witnesses of these things; and so is the Holy Spirit whom God has *given* to those who obey Him. (Acts 5:32 various versions)

Peter and John . . . prayed for them (Samaritans) that they might *receive* the Holy Spirit; For as yet He had not fallen upon any of them; they simply had been baptized in the name of the Lord Jesus. Then they laid their hands on them and they *received* the Holy Spirit. (Acts 8:14–17 various versions)

And when Simon saw that the Holy Spirit was *given* through the laying on of the apostles' hands, he offered them money, saying, Give me this power also, that whomever I lay hands on, he may *receive* the Holy Spirit. But Peter said to him, Your money perish with you because you thought the *gift* of God could be purchased. (Acts 8:18–20 various versions)

The Jewish believers who had come with Peter were astonished, because the *gift* of the Holy Spirit had been poured out upon the Gentiles also, for they heard them speak with tongues and magnify God. Then Peter asked, Can anyone object to their being baptized in water now that they have *received* the Holy Spirit just as we did ourselves? (Acts 10:45–47 various versions)

Since God *gave* them the same *Gift* that He gave us who believe on the Lord Jesus Christ, who was I to stand in God's way? (Acts 11:17 various versions)

Then Paul said unto them (Ephesian disciples of John), Did you *receive* the Holy Spirit when you believed? . . . And when Paul laid his hands upon them the Holy Ghost came upon them and they all spoke in tongues and prophesied. (Acts 19:2,6 various versions)

FULFILLMENT OF THE FATHER'S PROMISE

From the passages above, we find that the personal fulfillment of the Father's promise involves on the manward side four basic steps or phases:

1. There must be an *awareness* or *recognition* of need for the fullness of God's Holy Spirit. Jesus said that it is those who hunger and thirst after righteousness who shall be filled (Matt. 5:6).
2. One must *ask* for or *request* the Gift of the Holy Spirit in faith and obedience. There is an initiative which is necessary. This may involve the laying on of hands.

3. The Gift of the Spirit must be actively *appropriated* or *received*. Faith in the Father's promise brings the infilling presence which precludes faithless begging and pleading for a gift that has already been given.
4. One must *act* upon or *respond* to the Gift that has been received. What better response could there be than that of Spirit-directed praise, worship, and thanksgiving.

Being informed of the Father's provision for our spiritual needs and desires creates a hunger within for the fullness of His Spirit. We are motivated by hope and faith to ask Him for His gracious gift. Restfully, but actively, we appropriate His Holy Spirit and obediently respond in praise. Our praise can be in the form of a heavenly tongue or language unknown to our natural mind. This is not a strange or unusual manifestation of the Spirit, but a lovely privilege filled with power and purpose. Primarily, it is an expression of faith in, and submission to, the unceasing Spirit of prayer and praise which now fills our very being. The apostle James informs us that the tongue is a most unruly member which no man can tame (James 3:8). Only the power of the Holy Spirit can control our lips and our lives.

The apostle Paul refers to our praying and singing in tongues as a form of spiritual prayer and song which lifts us beyond the limitations of our minds (I Cor. 14:2,14–15). This is a ministry of the Holy Spirit which enables us to break the natural-thought barrier. There are times when we don't know what to pray for as we ought. Through this power of spiritual prayer, our petitions can be perfected beyond the restrictions of our understanding (Rom. 8:26–27).

There is a sense in which this gift of divinely inspired prayer is an expression of the supremacy of the Spirit over the mind of man. Little wonder this manifestation is such an offense to the intellect. It speaks of humility before God and submission to His Spirit, both in the realm of thought and in the world of words. The power that can control the mind and harness the tongue can bridle the whole body (James 3:2).

Now we can better understand why God chose to repeatedly link the manifestation of tongues with receiving the Holy Spirit in His fullness (Acts 2:4; 10:45-46; 19:6). This is a response in which prayer expresses both faith (trust) and obedience (submission). These qualities find their source in love. We can completely trust in and submit to only those with whom we have a genuine love relationship.

The promise of the Father is a promise of love. The Gift of the Spirit is a gift of love. Love inspires hope and fosters faith. It also creates a desire to please one's beloved: "Your wish is my command." Love is the fountainhead from which flows the river of divine discipline and obedience. Love, faith, and obedience are the basic principles on the manward side which form the foundation for a full life in the Spirit.

PRINCIPLES IN PRACTICE

Obviously, we have here the means by which God's heavenly purpose for our earthly lives is to be fulfilled. How, in a practical way do these principles work? The transaction, in one sense, involves two parts—God's and man's. We can't play His part, and He won't play our part. We had best learn where the dividing line is located.

The story of Peter's midnight walk on the stormy waters of Galilee helped me to locate the dividing line when it came to finding my release regarding the devotional tongue of praise. I had limped along in many ways for some five years after receiving the Holy Spirit, because I didn't fully understand the principles of faith and obedience which enable us to move into our new life in the Spirit, and to move on. I don't mean to imply that there had been no progress at all, for in some areas it had been phenomenal, but there were some basic hang-ups from which I needed to be unhooked. Praying in tongues was the issue God chose to teach me the working principles which opened up subsequent areas of ministry beyond anything I could have anticipated.

I would like to share some of the lessons I learned from Peter's unusual excursion on the water (Matt. 14).

Jesus was facing a rather critical time in His ministry. The people as a whole were more interested in His miracles than they were in His message. They were soon to be disenchanted by His emphasis on the heavenly and spiritual qualities of the Kingdom which they hoped He would establish on earth. Many of His disciples were "to go back and walk no more with Him." Jesus was even prompted to inquire of the Twelve, "Will ye also go away?" Peter's response, "Lord, to whom shall we go? Thou hast the words of eternal life," indicates something had been planted in his life which had taken root. What had happened to Peter which had placed such a growing faith in his heart?

Jesus' question concerning the loyalty of His disciples occurred following a series of significant events:

1. Jesus commissioned the Twelve by twos to preach, teach, heal, and deliver with power and authority.
2. Jesus was informed of John the Baptist's death. He responded by taking the Twelve, upon their return, aside for a time of prayer, reflection, and teaching. He realized His own death was but a year away.
3. Jesus and the Twelve were intercepted by the crowd, who heard His teaching, witnessed His healing power, and were miraculously fed by five loaves and two fishes. The disciples missed the meaning of the miracle, however, for their minds were closed.
4. Jesus walked upon the water in the midst of an ensuing storm. Of the fearful disciples, only Peter participated in this manifestation of God's power and glory.
5. Jesus preached His sermon on the "Bread of Life"; but the

people were more interested in the earthly bread of the previous day, and many drew back to walk with Him no more.

KINGDOM TRUTH: PRESENTED AND TESTED

Obviously, the Lord was endeavoring to lift His disciples to a greater place of faith, initiative, and responsibility, as part of their preparation to continue the cause of the Kingdom after His departure. Although they had participated in the work of the Kingdom following their commissioning by Jesus, they had not laid hold of the principles upon which the Kingdom was to rest. They could not transfer Kingdom truth from one setting to another.

It was difficult for them to break the pattern of natural, earthly ways, unless specifically instructed by Jesus. The feeding of the five thousand is an interesting example. In the face of a rather obvious need, He suggested that the disciples assume the responsibility of feeding the crowd. You can almost see their jaws drop with astonishment. The "Who, me?" response was quickly followed by a recovery of composure which allowed them to counsel the Lord on how foolish and impractical His suggestion had been. Little did they know that their confidence in the King was being tested, for Jesus already knew what He was going to do (John 6:6).

How different the situation might have been if one of the disciples had been bold enough in faith to have enthusiastically replied, "Wonderful, Lord, we will do just that! What part do you want us to play in the miracle?" They had moved in faith and obedience when on the miracle-road of their previous mission, but when it came to a common earthly need like daily bread, they couldn't get off the ground.

Another testing time was in the offing, however. Perhaps the story would be different this time. Jesus instructed them to gather up the uneaten bread and fish, and to their delight, there were twelve baskets full of leftover miracles, one for each of them. Then the Lord instructed the disciples to return to the boat (baskets and all) and proceed to the other side of Galilee while He remained behind to pray. He was at a particularly pivotal point in His earthly ministry, and it was a crucial time for His disciples. He needed to commune with His Heavenly Father!

For the disciples, it was a restful conclusion to a busy and demanding day. Feeding five thousand people is no small task, and the disciples were ready to relax in their small ship as the cool, evening breeze filled their sails and carried them swiftly across the waters toward Capernaum. Jesus was deep in prayer as the twilight hour faded into the darkness of the night. Only the twinkling lights of nearby Bethsaida could be seen. Soon, however, this peaceful scene was to be replaced by the violence of a sudden storm.

I have sometimes wondered if the Adversary might not have utilized the fury of the elements at this particular time to unsettle the developing faith of the disciples. As the wind's intensity reached the proportions of a gale, it was necessary for the disciples to lower the sails and man the oars, lest their little boat be capsized by the angry waves. It was a terrifying situation, intensified by the physical distress of aching arms and burning lungs.

Had they missed God's will? No, they had obediently followed their Master's instructions. (There can be storms in the center of God's will.) I am sure they wished Jesus was with them. He knew how to handle the stormy seas; they had seen Him do it before. If only Jesus knew about their need—but the night was dark, and the shore had long-since faded from view.

All of us occasionally pass through shadowed valleys so dark and deep that we can no longer see the face of our Shepherd before us. The Psalmist declares, however, that "the night shineth as the day: the darkness and the light are both alike to thee" (Ps. 139:12). Although we can't see the Lord, He can see us! And so the record reads on this occasion: "Jesus saw that they were distressed in rowing, for the wind was against them" (Mark 6:48 RSV). Immediately our hearts surge with joyful expectation, and we long to shout our encouragement to the disciples to hold fast. Jesus is coming—He is on His way.

DIVINE DELAYS

At this point, a synthesis of the Gospel accounts indicates a strange response upon the part of the Lord: He didn't do anything! In fact, John's record (John 6:19) informs us that they rowed some twenty-five to thirty furlongs (three or four miles) before Jesus came to their aid. Matthew (14:25) tells us the time was about the fourth watch, between three and six o'clock in the morning. This means they had been toiling most of the night. Why did Jesus delay His rescue?

There are a number of what we might call "divine delays" in Scripture. (This is one; the death of Lazarus is another.) They make an interesting study, because each delay is related to divine purpose which was not apparent to those involved. What might have been the purpose in this delay is interesting to think about.

Perhaps the Lord was allowing them an opportunity to face the situation with faith rather than give way to fear. Just a glance at the back of the boat where the twelve baskets of leftover miracles were might have reminded them of the miracle-working power with which Jesus had commissioned them some weeks earlier. They had healed the sick, cast out devils, and preached the good news concerning the Kingdom. Could they translate that truth into their present plight?

What might have happened if they had called a prayer meeting in the middle of the storm and rebuked the wind as they had seen Jesus do so successfully some months earlier? But they didn't. Sometimes it is easier for us to move in faith when we are on an unusual mission for God (as the disciples were previously) than it is when we face the difficulties of more familiar settings (in our homes or at our work). Several of the disciples were seasoned professionals when it came to the wily ways of the sea. Maybe their knowledge was a hindrance to faith. Perhaps, too, it was well to have their natural strength and skill pressed to the limit. Somewhere along the line, self-sufficiency must give way to a confidence which rests solely in the Lord.

POWER OF HIS PRESENCE

Although Jesus could have stilled the storm from the shoreline, He chose to reassure their faltering faith by walking toward them on the water. His approach caused a remarkable response on the part of the disciples. We are told in Matthew's Gospel (14:26) that they were terrified and cried out in fear, for they thought they were seeing a ghost. Apparently they weren't expecting to see Jesus in the middle of their storm. (Are we?) He immediately encouraged them by identifying Himself and calming their fears. (It is one thing to be in distress, and quite another for distress to be in us.)

The Amplified Bible (Matt. 14:27) suggests that in the original language Jesus shouted across the waves these inspiring words: "Take courage! I AM; stop being afraid!" The "I AM" of Jesus should always evoke a ready response from every disciple: "Truly, THOU ART!"

The "I AM" of God was very real to David, as evidenced by the Twenty-third Psalm: "Yea, though I walk through the valley of the shadow of death, I will fear no evil: for—THOU ART—with me. . . ." Again in Psalm Sixteen we read, "I have set the Lord always before me: because—HE IS—at my right hand, I shall not be moved" (capitals mine).

LESSONS FROM PETER'S RESPONSE

Peter's response to the Word of the Lord was somewhat ambivalent. In his *head,* he questioned if the whole thing was for real—this is a time for cautious reflection and reasoned judgment. Yet in his *heart,* he knew it was the Lord, and he had a strange impulse to move from the role of a spectator to that of a participant. At long last there was somebody who was willing to make a leap of faith and join with Jesus in a performance of God's Word in power.

He shouted out above the storm that if this was really Jesus (that part was from his head), then might he come to the Lord upon the waters (that part was from his heart). Peter had the proper perspective. He didn't ask if he could walk on the water, too. (What a story that would make back home—Peter, the water-walker!) Rather, he requested that *he might come to Jesus*—upon the waters. If Jesus had not been in the center of the situation, there would have been no sense in walking on the water. It was the purpose His presence brought to the miracle which gave it value and meaning. This is true of all of God's miraculous gifts, including the heavenly tongue of praise.

Jesus replied immediately. He didn't give a long dissertation trying to prove His identity to Peter. He didn't suggest that Peter read a good ten-volume set on theology, or even a thorough scientific treatise on the physics of water-walking. He simply said, "Come!"

Peter was *aware* of his desire to be with Jesus on this occasion of God's glory and power (step number one). Then he *asked*

Jesus if he could be a participant (step number two). Jesus quickly responded by giving His Word. The next move was Peter's, not the Lord's. Someone once said that God is the fastest chess player in the world—it's always your move! Notice the interplay of parts as the scene unfolded. There was a part which only God could perform, but there was also a part which Peter had to play. He had to *accept* the Word which the Lord had given (step number three).

This is where so many of us fail. If we had been in Peter's place, we probably would have kept begging and pleading for permission to participate. "Oh, please, God. You don't know how great is my need, and how deep is my desire. I beg of You to be gracious and hear my pitiful plea. Please don't turn me aside. I can't go on without a sense of Your power in my life. Oh Lord, please give me some assurance that You have heard the cry of my heart. It is with agony of soul that I earnestly beseech Thee to be merciful. Please, Lord, oh please!"

Such a prayer can have noble qualities of honesty, sincerity, and persistence, but if prolonged, it can also assume the form of a faithless, frustrated petition. It certainly never would have walked Peter on the water. Many times I have talked with people who have been seeking the "promise of the Father" for years, but who have never realized it was their responsibility to *accept* the given gift with an attitude of thanksgiving.

Peter apparently accepted the Lord's invitation without question. His next move was to *act* on the given word (step number four). It is at this point that some of us have difficulty. This was my parking place for five years. In sharing with others, I have discovered there are a whole host of questions and reservations which can keep us in the boat. Again, let us consider what might have happened if we had been in Peter's place with our problems.

Mr. Caution would probably have told the Lord to hold it a minute because he felt this was really a time for some careful consideration and counsel. A hasty move at this point might involve some unforeseen problems, since this was somewhat of an unbeaten path. Perhaps the disciples could organize themselves into a committee and analyze the whole situation from a theological and psychological perspective!

Mr. Fearful would have been already conditioned by a lifetime of warning concerning the dangers of deep-sea duty. It just wasn't the tradition of seafaring men to go leaping into the waters of a storm-lashed lake in the middle of the night. There were all kinds of strange stories circulating around the lakeside towns of men who had been caught by sudden winds and never returned. It really would be much wiser to stay in the boat with the other disciples. A well-made boat is the safest place to be in stormy weather. There was no doubt about the ship's construction. It had been made and maintained by the family for years and years.

Mr. Play-It-Cool probably would have assured Jesus how much he appreciated the invitation to join Him on the lake. There was no doubt in his mind about the identity of the Lord or the validity of the experience. In fact he would be pleased to personally encourage anyone who might express an interest in that direction. Goodness knows, the world needs men who are courageous enough to walk on the water. However, if it's just the same to Jesus, he would prefer to remain in the boat and cheer everybody on from where he was.

Mr. Pride would immediately have pictured the whole scene of water-walking from the perspective of the onlooking disciples and the stories they would circulate when they returned home. No one likes to be considered a foolish fanatic, and there isn't a quicker way to get the label than to go walking on the water in the middle of a storm. How could he explain to anybody that anything that bizarre could be of God? They would probably think the strain of the storm had unsettled his mind, and he had become hysterical and lost his emotional balance. He had lost enough respect when he had chosen to follow Jesus. This was carrying things too far.

Mr. Timid-But-Determined would have forced himself to the side of the boat, and after carefully adjusting his water wings, would have hesitantly eased himself to the water's surface. With both hands firmly grasping the boat, he repeatedly tested the firmness of the water with his feet. In his mind was the thought of tiptoeing his way out a few steps and then seeing how he thought and felt about the whole thing. It just wasn't his nature to abandon himself to anything without cautiously testing it out inch-by-inch as he proceeded. We might suppose that after a number of false starts, he might eventually make it—if the storm didn't get any worse, or the disciples in the boat didn't talk him out of it.

Mr. Passive-Pious would have initially viewed the entire scene with mild interest. He didn't want to miss anything that really was of the Lord, but this didn't really fit well with his concept of divine wisdom. Then, too, there was a disturbing element of sensationalism that was foreign to his preference for reverence when in the presence of God. This just didn't seem like the right time, place, or procedure for a holy work of the Spirit. Surely everybody doesn't have to walk on the water to prove their faith and love for God. The Lord works so differently with each one; it is foolish even to think that everyone has to fit into the same pattern. Still, if there was some remote possibility this was a privilege for all of the disciples, he didn't want to turn his back on the whole thing. In an endeavor to resolve his conflict of interest, he undoubtedly came to the conclusion that if some day God really wanted him to walk on the water, he wouldn't turn the Lord down. In the meantime, it wasn't anything he would actively pursue. Day would be breaking soon, and a peaceful meditation at sunrise was something a little more in keeping with his tradition.

Mr. True-Blue would have quickly perceived this experience was going to be miraculous in its character. This was something that had to be God all the way through. One thing in which he had always prided himself was his sincerity and honesty before the Lord. He had a great fear of "getting in the flesh" or doing something on his own and saying it was God. He wasn't about to get psyched-up by swimming on the water's surface and then presumptuously proclaiming to everybody he had walked on the water. He was determined to be honest with himself and God. Nobody was going to call him a phony. There was just one way to be absolutely sure the experience would be real and unspoiled by the hand of man: He would announce to the Lord that he wanted the entire excursion to be 100 percent of God. He would not take any initiative or make a move on his own. If this was the will of the Lord, He could, by the supreme power of His Word, lift Mr. True-Blue from the boat and transport him across the waters to Himself. In this way they both would be certain the whole experience was of God. Furthermore, Mr. True-Blue would have preserved his pride concerning his purity of Spirit!

Then, of course, there is always Mr. Try-Anything. He always wanted to be where the action was, especially if it related to the unusual. He had made the rounds when it came to spiritual experiences, and walking on the water topped them all. If this was going to be the next fad in religious circles, he wanted to be one of the first to try it, and proudly display his charter-membership certificate. He needed no encouragement and seemed bothered by the suggestion that he might need further instruction concerning personal commitment, and the purpose for God's power in his life. The idea that waters are to be buried in as well as walked upon seemed particularly distasteful to him. Unable to restrain his enthusiasm any longer, he vaulted over the side of the boat opposite the bright presence of Jesus, and rushed headlong into the waiting waters and darkness of the deep.

AFTER THE LEAP IS MADE

If any of the above thoughts crossed Peter's mind, he must have quickly dismissed them, for the narrative indicates he acted immediately by both a *leap* and a *walk* of faith straight toward Jesus. In fact, he almost reached the Lord before his move was challenged. Up to that point, his eyes had been upon the welcoming hands of Jesus—the word "come" was still ringing in his ears. Then a thought familiar to us all flashed through his mind: "What have I gotten myself into!" Man will always have second thoughts following a leap of faith, and Peter was no exception. It seemed wise to re-evaluate the situation, and a glance at the stormy sea provided no comfort whatsoever. A great gust of wind hurled a huge wave in Peter's direction. Horrified by the howling storm, he hesitated, and fear filled his pounding heart—Peter, the rock, was about to sink like one.

If only he had not hesitated but maintained his steady steps of faith toward Jesus. Satan had repeatedly hardened the hearts and dulled the minds of the disciples concerning not only the spiritual character of the Kingdom, but also the power and authority of the King (Mark 6:52). Of the Twelve, only Peter had broken the pattern, and the Enemy is a hard loser. If he can't keep us from moving in, he will endeavor to keep us from moving on. Once more he pulled Peter's mind into the downward track of men's thinking, and his heart followed the same path.

In his desperation, Peter—with one last flash of faith—cried out to Jesus for help. Immediately the strong arm of the Lord raised Peter out of the depths and replanted his feet on the firm ground of His Word. After catching him, Jesus taught

Peter more perfectly concerning the consistency of true faith, and gave him one more opportunity to exercise his faith, as together they walked back to the boat through the storm.

A PERSONAL TESTIMONY

How readily we can sympathize with Peter in his plight, and find our hopes aroused by his victory. It was this story which helped me over my hurdle concerning prayer in the Spirit. I wasn't about to initiate something that was just of myself. Anybody could say nonsense syllables; such gibberish was nothing more than mechanical movements of the mouth. I wanted an all-of-God-none-of-me experience. But the Lord finally allowed me to see that my earthly way of analysis, far from being noble, was indicative of a hard heart that stubbornly refused to believe His Word.

Once my doubt was defined, I repented for faithlessly lingering in the boat, and prepared myself to leap forth in faith and walk out on the waters of prayer and praise. I confessed the indwelling and infilling presence of the Holy Spirit. I confessed that Jesus was altogether faithful and altogether worthy. I confessed that my leap of faith would involve the lifting of my voice in continuous sound; that although I initiated the movements of my tongue and lips producing syllables of praise not understood by my natural mind, the Holy Spirit was faithfully prompting and directing my utterance.

I informed my Heavenly Father that I was offering this, the fruit of my lips, as a sacrifice of praise from a heart of faith, love, and obedience. I purposed within that I would start and not stop (as did Peter) to see how I thought and felt about my venture. It was going to be life-giving "bread and fish," not "stones and serpents" that leave one feeling heavy and hurt, for my Father had faithfully promised.

The first little vowel-like sounds were soft and simple, but became increasingly fluent and articulate as I actively cooperated with the unceasing Spirit of praise and worship. I was aware of a warm feeling of release and relief—as if a time of inward struggle had come to a glorious conclusion. Throughout the weeks that followed, I continued to praise God all throughout each day as I went about my instructional duties at school. Praying in the Spirit became as natural as breathing—and indeed, it is, spiritually speaking, the breath of life!

On one occasion while I was praying in tongues for a woman who was depressed, she and a friend informed me that I was commanding her release in Spanish, a language I have never learned. The Lord reminded me of the evening when I first found my freedom in Spirit-prompted prayer and praise. I was impressed that if I had not made my move in faith then, the Spirit could not have made His move of encouragement, as He obviously had done, for my needy sister in Christ.

The principles of faith and obedience have since found application in many different directions in my life. We all will continually become aware of new needs and deeper desires in the Lord which bring us to our Heavenly Father. He is always ready to hear our requests and wants us to receive and respond to the appropriate answer of His choosing. Peter's walk on the water continues to be a source of inspiration as the storms of life suddenly arise even when we are in the midst of His will. Our life in the Spirit is not to be a weary sink-or-swim affair, but rather a refreshing walk in faith with God.

3

THE COMING OF THE COMFORTER

A Faithful Teacher

Comfort, oh, *comfort* my people, says your God. Speak tenderly to Jerusalem and tell her that her sad days are gone. Her sins are pardoned, and the Lord will give to her twice as many blessings as he gave her punishment before. . . . O Crier of Good News, shout to Jerusalem from the mountain tops! Shout louder—don't be .afraid—tell the cities of Judah, "Your God is *coming!*" Yes, the Lord God is *coming* with mighty power. . . . He will feed his flock like a shepherd; he will carry the lambs in his arms and gently lead the ewes with young. (Isa. 40:1, 9–11 TLB)

The Lord is my shepherd; I shall not want. . . . He leadeth me in the paths of righteousness for his name's sake. Yea, though I walk through the valley of the shadow of death, I will fear no evil: for thou art with me; thy rod and thy staff they *comfort* me. (Ps. 23:1,3–4)

If you love me, obey me; and I will ask the Father and He will give you another *Comforter* (Counselor, Helper, Intercessor, Advocate, Strengthener and Standby), and He will never leave you. He is the Holy Spirit, the Spirit who leads into all *truth.* . . . No, I will not abandon you or leave you *comfortless* (orphans, desolate, bereaved, forlorn and helpless). I will come back to you! (John 14:15–18; 16:13 various versions)

31

When the Father sends the *Comforter* in my name (in my place)—and by the *Comforter* I mean the Holy Spirit—He will *teach* you all things, as well as remind you of everything I myself have told you. (John 14:26 various versions)

I will send you the *Comforter*—the Holy Spirit, the source of all *truth.* He will *come* to you from the Father and will tell you all about me. (John 15:26 TLB)

Truly, it is best for you that I go away, for if I don't, the *Comforter* won't *come.* If I do, He will—for I will send Him to you, to be in close fellowship with you. . . . When the Spirit of *Truth* (truth-giving Spirit) comes, He will guide you into all *truth,* for He will not be presenting His own ideas, but will be passing on to you what He has heard from the Father. He will tell you about the future. He shall praise me and bring me great honor by showing (revealing, communicating, transmitting) to you my glory. (John 16:7, 13–14 various versions)

Meanwhile, the church had peace throughout Judea, Galilee and Samaria, and grew in strength and numbers. The believers *learned* how to walk in fear of the Lord and in the *comfort* of the Holy Spirit. (Acts 9:31 TLB)

Blessed be God, even the Father of our Lord Jesus Christ, the Father of mercies, and the God of all *comfort;* Who *comforteth* us in all our tribulation, that we may be able to *comfort* them which are in any trouble, by the *comfort* wherewith we ourselves are *comforted* of God (II Cor. 1:3–4)

Finally, brethren, farewell. Be perfect, be of good *comfort,* be of one mind, live in peace; and the God of love and peace be with you. . . . The grace of the Lord Jesus Christ, and the love of God, and the *communion* (fellowship, friendship, companionship) of the Holy Spirit be with you all. Amen. (II Cor. 13:11,14 various versions)

The divine ministry of comfort has roots which reach far back into the Old Testament. The Hebrew word for "comfort" is *nacham* and means, literally, "to give forth sighs" (as of sympathy and consolation). The Lord is the "God of all comfort," an attribute which David warmly personalizes as the Good Shepherd in his Twenty-third Psalm. The rod and staff refer to divine direction and protection during dark times of distress or decision. The redeeming love of God for His people is beautifully pictured in His many promises and provisions for Israel. She, of course, is a type of the church, and we come under the same tender care and concern as was her portion.

Introduced to the Holy Spirit

In the New Testament, the Lord Himself relates the ministry of comfort to the Person of the Holy Spirit. On the day before His death, Jesus spent much time in carefully introducing the disciples to the Holy Spirit, who was soon to come, following His ascension (John 14:15-16). The Person and work of the Holy Spirit was presented as being of supreme importance, more important even than His own physical presence with them. Jesus told His bewildered and saddened followers that He was going to leave them—but not alone. He promised to send them another Comforter like unto Himself, but without the limitations of a physical body. The Holy Spirit would be the Lord's personal representative here on earth. He not only was going to be *with* them, but *in* them, all the time, and everywhere. What a foreign and fantastic thought that must have been to the listening disciples!

Like many of us, the Twelve probably had a difficult time trying to confer personality on a description which seemed so "ghostly"! The concepts of divine fatherhood and sonship were more easily grasped, for there were comparable relationships in their earthly families. But what kind of a familiar earthly figure can you put the Holy Spirit into? In about fifty days (Pentecost) they were to experience the answer to their question. In fact, they would be the answer—each life was to become a temple in which the Holy Spirit would personally abide and reproduce this life of Jesus.

In their new relationship with the Holy Spirit, they discovered He had, indeed, all of the characteristics of personality. He was far more than just a divine power, force, or influence; He was a powerful, forceful, influential Person, with whom they enjoyed intimate fellowship.

As to His "Person," the Lord Jesus is at the right hand of the Father, but it is the ministry of the Holy Spirit to indwell each believer with His "Presence." In other words, God's Spirit personally *reveals* Jesus to us, *realizes* Jesus in us, and *releases* Jesus through us. After His ascension, the Lord continued and extended His earthly ministry by indwelling each member of His Body with the same Spirit that motivated Him. The Spirit that revealed the Father to the Son now reveals the Son to the believer.

If we are going to have communion (fellowship) with the Holy Spirit, there will be one life-transforming topic of conversation—Jesus. He will not be interested in discussion that is unrelated ultimately to the Lord. Some have expressed a concern that in honoring the Holy Spirit, we may be depreciating the Person of Christ. They fail to appreciate the ministry of the Spirit. If we truly honor the Holy Spirit, He will honor Jesus; if we make room for the Holy Spirit, He immediately will make room for the Lord. Actually, to ignore the many ministries of the Spirit is to frustrate the Father's desire to manifest His Son to and through our lives. There is no other way.

There is a sense in which God the Father, through the hidden ministry of the Holy Spirit, introduces us to Jesus as our Savior, and we thereby enter into a new life relationship with Him:

No man can come to me, except the Father which hath sent me draw him. (John 6:44)

And when he [the Holy Spirit] is come, he will reprove [convict, convince] the world of sin, and of righteousness, and of judgment. (John 16:8)

You are controlled by your new nature if you have the Spirit of God living in you. (And remember that if anyone doesn't have the Spirit of Christ living in him, he is not a Christian at all.) (Rom. 8:9 TLB)

In other words, the Father, by the Spirit and through the Son, draws us to Himself. He takes the initiative in restoring our family relationship which was broken by man's rebellion (sin). By the Holy Spirit, we are convicted of our sin, convinced we need to be saved from that sin, and are shown our Savior in Christ Jesus. In receiving Christ into our lives, we are indwelt with the Holy Spirit, who then fills our lives with the presence of Christ. The Spirit Himself is the one who makes Jesus very real to us in a warm and personal way.

There is also a sense in which Jesus now wants to introduce us to the indwelling Person of the Holy Spirit that we might know and understand, not only His life-giving, but also His power-releasing ministry. It is one thing to have entered into a life-relationship with Jesus, but quite another to appropriate the power necessary to fully express it. The coming of the Comforter is to provide strength and wisdom for our Christian walk. The Holy Spirit is a very practical Person with whom we need to become better acquainted.

I remember the night that my wife was baptized in the Holy Spirit by Jesus, something happened which deeply impressed me concerning the gracious and gentle Person-to-person relationship which is involved.

It was something of a miracle that she even consented to come to another home meeting, for in my zeal I had been pushing her as hard as I could toward the tender Dove of God's Spirit. I noticed He kept flying away every time I thought I had them in the same cage. I finally realized He is a very gentle Person, and will not violate the privacy of our personality. He patiently hovers over our lives waiting for *our* invitation before winging His way into our hearts.

After I finally gave up, my wife readily gave in; that same night she earnestly sought the Promise of her Heavenly Father. As a visiting minister laid hands upon her head and prayed that Jesus would quench her spiritual thirst with refreshing streams of living water, the Holy Spirit graced her life in a most beautiful way. As she began responding in heavenly praise and worship, the minister said, "Oh, He has come; the Blessed Comforter has come, and He has come to stay!"

There was something so warm and personal about those unforgettable words. This was more than just an emotional experience; it was the beginning of a companionship with her Blessed Comforter that was going to last forever. How pleased the Holy Spirit must be when we choose to be embraced by His loving Presence. How He longs for our fellowship in Christ Jesus: "The Spirit which He has made to dwell in us jealously desires us" (James 4:5 NASB margin).

His Personal Ministry

So often we have a tendency to depersonalize the Holy Spirit without realizing that in so doing we miss something of His tender touch upon our lives. Although the Greek word for "spirit" is a *neuter* noun, most passages relating to the Holy Spirit employ *personal* pronouns:

But when *He,* the Spirit of truth, comes, *He* will guide . . . *He* will speak . . . *He* will disclose . . . *He* shall glorify me. (John 16:13–14 NASB)

And while they were ministering to the Lord and fasting, the Holy Spirit said, "Set apart for *Me* Barnabas and Saul for the work to which *I* have called them." (Acts 13:2 NASB, italics mine)

The Holy Spirit is personally interested and involved in bringing each of us into a true living relationship with the Lord Jesus Christ. Notice the diversity of ministry and personal activity in the following passages:

1. He strives with man (Gen. 6:3).
2. He instructs us in our wilderness experiences (Neh. 9:20).
3. He protects us from the Enemy (Isa. 59:19).
4. He causes us to rest when we are weary (Isa. 63:14).
5. He causes us to walk in God's ways (Ezek. 36:27; Gal. 5:25).
6. He ministers life and quickens us (Ezek. 37:14; Job 33:4; John 6:33; Rom. 8:11; I Pet. 3:18).
7. He pours Himself out upon us (Joel 2:28; Acts 2:17-18; Acts 10:45).
8. He empowers the weak (Micah 3:8; Luke 24:49; Acts 1:8; II Tim. 1:7).
9. He leads the sons of God (Matt. 4:1; Rom. 8:14).
10. He speaks to and through us (Matt. 10:20; I Tim. 4:1; Heb. 3:7; Rev. 2:7; 14:13; 22:17).
11. He delivers us from demon power (Matt. 12:28).
12. He overshadows the humble and obedient (Luke 1:35).
13. He teaches us (Luke 12:12; John 14:26; I Cor. 2:13).
14. He regenerates us—attends our spiritual birth (John 3:5; Titus 3:5).
15. He refreshes the thirsty (John 7:37-39).
16. He comforts the bereaved and lonely (John 14:16, 18).
17. He testifies to us of Jesus (John 15:26).
18. He reproves the world (John 16:8).
19. He guides us into all truth (John 16:13).
20. He gives divine utterance to those who wish to sing, pray, and worship in the Spirit (Acts 2:4; 10:45-46; I Cor. 14:15; Eph. 6:18; Jude 20).
21. He gives boldness for us to witness (Acts 4:31).
22. He fills us with faith (Acts 6:5; 11:24).
23. He ordains and approves the servants of God (Acts 13:2-4; 20:28; II Cor. 6:4, 6).

24. He fills us with joy in spite of circumstances (Acts 13:52; I Thess. 1:6).
25. He forbids and restrains us in times of decision (Acts 16:6–7).
26. He sheds His love in our hearts (Rom. 5:5; 15:30; Col. 1:8; II Tim. 1:7).
27. He liberates our lives (Rom. 8:2; II Cor. 3:17; Isa. 61:1).
28. He prompts within us the heart-cry, "Abba, Father" (Rom. 8:15; Gal. 4:6).
29. He brings His witness concerning our sonship (Rom. 8:16; I John 5:6).
30. He intercedes on our behalf (Rom. 8:26).
31. He fills our lives with joy, peace, and hope (Rom. 15:13).
32. He justifies and sanctifies each believer (Rom. 15:16; I Cor. 6:11; II Thess. 2:13; I Pet. 1:2).
33. He confirms our ministry of God's Word by signs and miracles (Rom. 15:19; I Cor. 2:4; I Thess. 1:5; Heb. 2:4).
34. He searches out and reveals to us divine mysteries (I Cor. 2:9–10; Eph. 3:5).
35. He indwells (inhabits) our lives—temples (I Cor. 3:16; 6:19; Eph. 2:22).
36. He bestows spiritual gifts upon us (I Cor. 12:4–11; Heb. 2:4).
37. He officially seals our lives for God (II Cor. 1:22; Eph. 1:13; 4:30).
38. He is the earnest of our full spiritual inheritance (II Cor. 1:22; 5:5; Eph. 1:13–14).
39. He writes the letter-of-life upon our hearts (II Cor. 3:3, 6).
40. He transforms us into the image of Christ (II Cor. 3:18).
41. He communes (fellowships) with us (II Cor. 13:14; Phil. 2:1).
42. He opposes the works of the flesh in our lives (Gal. 5:16–17).
43. He produces in us the fruit of the spirit (Gal. 5:22; Eph. 5:9).
44. He provides for us an access through Jesus to the Father (Eph. 2:18).
45. He strengthens us in the inner man (Eph. 3:16).
46. He produces a peaceful unity among the brethren (Eph. 4:3).
47. He fills our lives with melody (Eph. 5:18–19).
48. He sharpens the sword of God's Word in our hand (Eph. 6:17; Heb. 4:12).
49. He supplies the "turning power" which redirects adversity for our salvation (Phil. 1:19).
50. He warns us concerning end-time deception (I Tim. 4:1).

51. He stimulates in us sound, balanced, disciplined thinking (II Tim. 1:7).
52. He enables us to keep the good things (treasures) of God without loss (II Tim. 1:14).
53. He provides us with God's prophetic word (II Pet. 1:21; Rev. 19:10).
54. He invites us to freely drink from the water of life (Rev. 22:17).

PERSONALITY CHARACTERISTICS

The various activities of the Holy Spirit involve *thought, feeling, purpose,* and *memory,* all of which are attributes of personality. Furthermore, the Spirit not only "acts" as a person, but can be "acted upon" as a person:

1. He can be spoken and sinned against (Matt. 12:31–32).
2. He can be lied to (Acts 5:3).
3. He can be tempted—provoked (Acts 5:9).
4. He can be resisted (Acts 7:51).
5. He can be quenched—suppressed, stifled (I Thess. 5:19).
6. He can be done despite—insulted, mocked, outraged (Heb. 10:29).

The Holy Spirit can also "react" as a person:

1. He can be vexed (Isa. 63:10).
2. He can be grieved—offended, hurt, saddened (Eph. 4:30).

Many of the ministries of the Holy Spirit surely must reflect the emotional side of His personality as well:

1. Only a *lovely* person can minister *love* (Rom. 5:5; 15:30; Gal. 5:22; II Tim. 1:7).
2. Only a *joyful* person can minister *joy* (Acts 13:52; Rom. 14:17; 15:13; Gal. 5:22).
3. Only a *peaceful* person can minister *peace* (Rom. 14:17; 15:13; Gal. 5:22; Eph. 4:3; Rev. 1:4).
4. Only a *hopeful* person can minister *hope* (Rom. 15:13).

As the executive member of the Godhead, the Holy Spirit is the one who performs (executes, actualizes) the will of the Father. He acts with both understanding and feeling. Surely it was with intense interest and expectation that He "brooded" (mother-movements) over the face of the waters in the early hours of creation. Then God spoke: "Let there be light"; with the Word went the Spirit—and light flashed into existence!

The crowning act of creation was later initiated by these sublime words: "Let us make man in our own image." Fashioned from the earth, man had *breathed* into him the "spirit" of life; and man became a living soul. Heavenly purpose was brought to birth through the "actualizing" power of the Holy Spirit! The wonder of God's wisdom was gloriously expressed and became the occasion for great joy in the heavens (Prov. 8:31–32; Job 38:5–7).

Would not the same feeling and interest accompany the divine miracle of creation by which we become new creatures in Christ Jesus?

> For the same God who ordered light to shine in darkness has flooded our hearts with His light that we might be shown the glory of God as we see it in the face of Jesus Christ. . . . And all of us have no veils upon our faces, but reflect like mirrors the glory of the Lord into whose image we are being changed with ever-increasing splendor. This transformation comes from the Lord who is the Spirit. (II Cor. 4:6; 3:18 various versions)

The Holy Spirit must find great delight in reproducing the life of Jesus throughout the family of the Father. In fact, a study of the word "joy" as it relates to the members of the Godhead seems to indicate that it is a response which is shared by them all. They rejoice together and desire that we share in that pleasure with them.

The Scriptures declare that there is much happiness in heaven when the lost is found, and the Enemy's hold on a life is broken (Luke 15:6–7). It is the purpose of God's Spirit to minister deliverance, freedom, and healing (Isa. 61:1–3), and what an occasion for great joy this becomes for the Holy Trinity:

> Sing, O daughter of Zion; shout, O Israel; be glad and rejoice with all the heart, O daughter of Jerusalem. The Lord hath taken away thy judgments, he hath cast out thine enemy: the king of Israel, even the Lord, is in the midst of thee: thou shalt not see evil any more. . . . The Lord thy God in the midst of thee is mighty; he will save, he will rejoice over thee with joy; he will rest in his love, he will joy over thee with singing. (Zeph. 3:14–15, 17)

One day while I was in the middle of conducting a Bible study, the Holy Spirit moved in an unusual and interesting way. The topic concerned the releasing power which can come to our lives through the Baptism in the Holy Spirit. Suddenly a rather gracious and composed young woman began to laugh almost uncontrollably. It was an appealing, lilting laughter which became quite contagious (although at a more subdued level) throughout the entire class. I recall chuckling sympathetically along with everyone else; then I noticed that my laughter was becoming louder and more hilarious than I could account for in the natural. Such behavior is not usually associated with professional dignity, especially when the entire discussion is being taped.

The reason the two of us were so unusually moved by a flood of inward joy was discovered after class. The young woman had been greatly burdened by an unhealthy obsession with demonic activity. Preoccupation with the devil and his activities can cloud our vision of the Lordship of Jesus if pursued in a soulish way. I, too, had been praying for a balanced approach to deliverance and was discovering God has many ways of releasing His people which we need to appreciate and appropriate. The strong emphasis on our "liberty in the Spirit" (which we will discuss in another chapter) had lifted her burden and filled her with joy.

The Lord used the occasion, moreover, to teach us further concerning the personality of the Holy Spirit. There is a sense in which He, too, is filled with joy, and we are the only natural means He has of manifesting that joy. I had never thought of the Holy Spirit as laughing. I knew He could be grieved and saddened, but I had never before fully appreciated His sense of hilarious joy on the occasion of our release from spiritual bondage.

For several weeks thereafter, the same phenomenon occurred whenever the "Spirit of heaviness and mourning" was exchanged for the "garment of praise and the oil of joy" (Isa. 61:3). I recognized then why my natural response to seeing people set free following prayer was a spontaneous rise of joy and laughter. I was participating in the Lord's very own joy.

The principle carries over to other areas. There is a righteous anger and holy hatred for the Enemy and his cohorts and their evil ways. There are many references to the Lord's wrath, indignation, and anger in Scripture and its expression through God's servants.

He [God] let loose upon them [the Egyptians] the fierceness of His *anger, wrath* and *indignation,* and *distress,* by sending . . . angels of calamity and woe among them. (Ps. 78:49 TAB, italics mine)

Do not I [David] *hate* them, O Lord, who hate You? And am I not *grieved* and do not I *loathe* those who rise up against You? I *hate* them with perfect *hatred;* they have become my enemies. (Ps. 139:21–22 TAB, italics mine)

And He [Jesus] glanced around at them [Pharisees] with *vexation* and *anger, grieved* at the hardening of their hearts. (Mark 3:5 TAB, italics mine)

Righteous anger is not derived from a sense of personal offense coupled with a desire for personal retaliation. This is a soulish reaction and not a response of the Spirit at all. Holy hatred is directed toward the evil influence and power behind cruel and unjust conduct. This may require opposing those involved, but with a redemptive purpose in view. Jesus overthrew the money changers in the temple, and many times opposed the Pharisees with razor-sharp words of rebuke, yet always with a sense of grief in His heart (Matt. 23:1–39).

The anger, compassion, and releasing authority of the Holy Spirit can rise strong in the lives of God's servants on behalf of others in times of personal pain and distress.

I remember a student in my office breaking down in tears on one occasion because of a tragic incident which occurred in her early childhood. She had been molested by a relative, and the episode had left a fear in her heart that this would forever exclude her from the beauty and purity of a marriage with God's full blessing. She was afraid she would never be acceptable in the eyes of any young man who had waited for the girl of God's choosing.

There rose up within me a great sense of compassion which brought tears to my eyes. At the same time I felt an intense, holy anger in my heart toward the Enemy, who for years had tormented one of the Lord's loveliest children. With a great sense of divine authority, I opposed the cruel spirit of fear and torment, and the yoke of many years was broken. The Lord healed the wound and filled her life with the light of His love. (Incidentally, she now has a lovely Christian home and family.)

I realize now my emotional response of compassion and anger were reflections of what the Holy Spirit Himself was feeling. With the inward response came the power and authority for release. The Spirit of God desired to express Himself through me in manifesting the healing love of Jesus. I am sure many of you have had similar experiences in your response to spiritual needs. They enable us to appreciate the personality of the Holy Spirit—a most understanding and affectionate Person.

THE HOLY SPIRIT: OUR PARAKLETOS

The word "Comforter" in the Greek language has a range of meaning which in New Testament usage indicates a progressive ministry of the Holy Spirit designed for our maturity. Literally, the Greek term for "Comforter" (*Parakletos*) means one who is called alongside for assistance; in other words, a helper. The word was often used in connection with public servants. In the legal realm, the "parakletos" referred to a lawyer, counselor, advocate, adviser, defender, or prisoner's friend—one who could officially and effectively intercede on behalf of the accused. The word is used in I John 2:1, where Jesus Christ the righteous is referred to as the sinner's Advocate with the Father. "He ever liveth to make intercession for them" (Heb. 7:25).

The Holy Spirit becomes the intercessor for any of God's children who are in need. All of us from time to time become bewildered in mind and heavy of heart. How comforting it is to know there is Someone who can lift us beyond the limitations of our understanding and feelings. Paul knew what it was like to feel totally inadequate, even in prayer. He also knew the adequacy of the Holy Spirit on such occasions:

So, too, the Holy Spirit comes to our aid and supports us in our weakness; for we do not know what we ought to pray: but the Spirit Himself makes intercession for us with sighings too deep for words. And He who knows the hearts of men knows the mind of the Spirit, because He always pleads for the saints in harmony with God's will! (Rom. 8:26–27 various versions)

One way in which this intercessory ministry of the Spirit is accomplished is through our heavenly prayer language. Praying in tongues is a means of moving beyond the limitations of the intellect or confusions of the mind. As an expression of faith, it can lift us above the hurt and pain of a wounded heart. It is a great comfort and consolation to know the Holy Spirit can perfect our prayers of confession, petition, and intercession. He will prompt, perfect, and present our prayers to God precisely in accord with His will.

There have been times of agony in soul when I felt I had really grieved the will of the Lord, and could only rest in the faithfulness of the Holy Spirit to effectively present my prayer of repentance. On other occasions, when facing baffling situations and painful decisions, I have groaned and sighed in the Spirit, trusting Him to intercede with feeling on my behalf. On the more positive side, what strength and encouragement one can receive, when facing an opportunity to minister to others, by recognizing that our blessed Comforter is willing to prepare the hearts and lives of all involved as we yield to Him in prayer.

One night on my way to a prayer meeting in a home, I was really attacked by the Accuser concerning a minor incident in my life years ago. I felt a heavy compulsion to make a vow concerning a letter I was to write, or else I could not expect God's blessing on the forthcoming meeting. It is kind of a panicky feeling to think God is threatening to lift His Spirit, when He is the only confidence you have when facing such an opportunity. Furthermore, I was deeply impressed I was going to confront something most unusual for which I would not be prepared. I had about ten minutes to go before arrival.

How thankful I am for the faithfulness of our Heavenly Companion. He graciously gave me a word of wisdom: I was not to make any kind of a vow under duress unless I was absolutely sure it was the voice of God! I knew the Lord wouldn't speak in a dark, heavy, compulsive way, but the persistence of this accusation concerning my past was rather persuasive. I finally told the Lord I would write a thousand letters when I was sure this was His will, but until then, I would not make a vow concerning one word. I then confessed the forgiving, cleansing, redeeming power in the blood of Jesus, and fervently prayed in the Spirit for the forthcoming meeting.

When I arrived, it was to a most unexpected situation: the husband of the hostess had complained of not feeling well earlier in the evening and had suddenly stopped breathing. I immediately went into the bedroom, and as I gazed at his lifeless form, my first reaction was, "This is the situation I had been warned I would not be ready for." My second response was, "The past is under the blood of Jesus, and the Spirit Himself has prepared the path before us!"

The events of the entire evening involved many people and unusual demands for God's wisdom. What the Enemy had designed as an occasion of confusion, fear, and defeat became in the following weeks an opportunity for a beautiful testimony concerning the grace and faithfulness of God in the time of great personal need. Out of death in the natural, the Lord brought forth many springs of "living water."

Yes, the Holy Spirit truly is our Comforter. It is, indeed, a consolation to receive His counsel and support during times of great distress. The comfort He brings is more than consolation, however; it is also a source of strength and support which enables one to stand on his feet and face life. This ministry of the Spirit is not at all a sympathy that fosters self-pity; rather it is a compassion that puts steel in our soul.

There is an even stronger meaning to the word "comfort" which involves *encouragement, exhortation,* and *challenge.* In the verb form it was used with regard to exhorting troops about to go into battle—a rally-call. An encourager would put courage into the fainthearted, and nerve the feeble arm for fight, one who would make a very ordinary man cope gallantly with a perilous and dangerous situation (William Barclay, *New Testament Words*. London: SCM Press, 1964).

This, of course, is the whole theme of the Acts of the Apostles. Very ordinary men were used in most extraordinary ways for the cause of the Kingdom. They all knew persecution, peril, and even death; they also knew the Comforter personally. For this reason, "they were more than conquerors amid all of these things and gained a surpassing victory through Him who loved them" (Rom. 8:37 various versions).

The progression of meaning which the word "Comforter" holds for us can be developed in the following descriptions:

THE HOLY SPIRIT:
1. Defends us when we are helpless. (Our Defender).
2. Consoles us when we are sorrowful (Our Consoler).
3. Befriends us when we are lonely. (Our Friend).
4. Heals us when we are hurt. (Our Healer).
5. Refreshes us when we are weary. (Our Refresher).
6. Encourages us when we are depressed. (Our Encourager).
7. Steadies us when we are uncertain. (Our Stabilizer).
8. Strengthens us when we are weak. (Our Strengthener).
9. Informs us when we are ignorant. (Our Teacher).
10. Steels our soul when we are pressured. (Our Reinforcer).
11. Challenges us to be more than conquerors! (Our Captain).

It is the purpose of our blessed Comforter to move us toward maturity. Initially He protects and defends us—then He heals and strengthens us. After sufficient instruction, the Spirit encourages and charges us to now minister to the needs of others in His divine power and wisdom!

OUR INSTRUCTOR: THE SPIRIT OF TRUTH

The term "comforter" is repeatedly related by Jesus to the phrase, "Spirit of truth" (John 14:16–17). The Lord promised not to leave His disciples "orphans" or "comfortless," but He would send to them a divine Instructor who would abide in them and teach them all things pertaining to the Father's ultimate purpose for them in Christ Jesus.

Basically there is a restlessness (discomfort) to life which can be satisfied only by finding the peace which comes in a right and real relationship between ourselves and others. Inherent in truth are the qualities of rightness and realness. But how can we be true to ourselves and others if we don't even know what truth is? For many, truth is an arbitrary abstraction too blurred in their thinking to set a straight line for their lives.

When Pilate was confronted by Jesus at His trial, there rose up within him a mixed set of emotions. He was intrigued and annoyed—fascinated and provoked. He could not keep the situation objective, but was being strangely pulled into a position of personal involvement. Error is uncomfortable in the presence of truth. Pilate had the uneasy feeling he was facing Someone who was more real than he wanted to believe He was.

Partly serious, but mainly evasive, after the Lord's testimony concerning Himself, he raised the age-old question, "What is truth?" It was his moment of truth—his appointment for eternal life—and he missed it. The record reads that after his question he immediately went out again unto the Jews. He was within touching distance of the One-True-God, yet he turned away.

Spiritual truth, like eternal life, has to be translated into terms which we as creatures of earth and time can understand. Otherwise such concepts are rather vague, abstract, and coldly impersonal. For this reason, the Son of God clothed Himself in a warm, touchable garment of flesh through which He could reveal to man what God was really like. Since man was created in His image, this revelation also portrayed the quality of life which man was intended to live as God originally had planned it.

The life of Jesus is a two-way mirror which reveals God's glory and our destiny. In Christ we find the true pattern for the abundant and everlasting life. The Father's will and purpose center in His Son and reach forth to encompass an entire family of sons and daughters who are conformed into His image (Rom. 8:29). It is the desire of the Holy Spirit to transform our lives like unto His.

> Where the Spirit of the Lord is, there is liberty. We all can be mirrors that openly behold and reflect the glory of the Lord. We are transfigured in ever-increasing splendor into His own image, and the transformation comes from the Lord who is the Spirit. (II Cor. 3:17–18 various versions)

Jesus was truly, uniquely, and honestly Himself. To be conformed into His image is to discover our true selfhood as well. Furthermore, the Holy Spirit provides the necessary power for the release in Christ of our full personality potential as intended by our Heavenly Father. To be in Christ involves, among other things, a relationship with other members of His Body. We truly find ourselves as we find our place in the Body of Christ and our function in the family of God.

The Holy Spirit wishes to blend our natural God-given talents with His own special and selected gifts that we might be well-prepared for our particular ministry in the Lord. The apostle Paul expresses this nicely in one of his epistles:

> Naturally there are different gifts and functions; individually, grace is bestowed upon us in different ways out of the rich diversity of Christ's giving. . . . His gifts were given that Christians might be properly equipped for their service, that the whole Body be built up to a position of strength and maturity; until finally we come into a common faith and knowledge of the Son of God, and all become full-grown in the Lord—that

completeness of personality which is measured by the perfection of Christ's character. (Eph. 4:7, 12–13 various versions)

The Holy Spirit as our divine Instructor will teach us the truth about ourselves, and our relationship with God and with others. He desires that:

> We . . . no longer be like children, forever changing our minds about what we believe because someone has told us something different, or has cleverly lied to us and made the lie sound like the truth. Instead, we will lovingly follow the truth at all times—speaking truly, dealing truly, living truly—and so become more and more in every way like Christ who is the Head of his body, the church. (Eph. 4:14–15 TLB)

Honesty toward Others—God—Ourselves

There is a basic honesty which the Spirit of truth will bring to our lives. No longer need we be pious pretenders. I recall a popular song in the fifties entitled, "The Great Pretender." Probably all of us at one time or another could claim that label. We learn at an early age to layer our lives with an acceptable surface. Conversation and conduct are calculated in terms of social approval and respect.

Obviously it is neither necessary or desirable to bare our soul all the time, to everyone; this would violate the privacy and dignity of our selfhood. There are also social graces and common courtesies which ease the unavoidable friction occasioned by lives in contact with one another. We don't really expect everybody to unload all their woes and ills every time someone says, "How do you do?" On the other hand, to feel we have to continually cover over our true feelings and thinking lest we lose the love and respect of our peers borders on hypocrisy. This is not a malicious deception, but a protective device based on fear.

Such a deceptive attitude toward people, however, carries over into our relationship with God. We very seldom actually tell the Lord we don't feel like praying, worshiping, or reading the Bible, lest we invoke His displeasure—as if He doesn't know anyway. The Spirit of Truth would prompt us to be honest with God concerning our attitudes, for He can faithfully direct us to the cause of our indifference.

If we have grieved the Lord in thought, word, or deed, the Spirit will convince us of our need to clear the matter by specific confession of our sin. At the same time, He reveals to us our Savior and assures us of our forgiveness, thereby frustrating the devil's desire to accuse and condemn us. Hereby the joy of our salvation is restored.

Should our apparent apathy be based in natural weariness, the Spirit would encourage us to find our rest in the Lord, allowing Him to minister to us in our need. The Enemy seeks to pervert our concept of prayer and worship into a legal, formal function which is a lifeless chore. It is possible to worship the Lord in our work, rest, and recreation when our lives are filled with the unceasing Spirit of praise. Sometimes the Holy Spirit will purposely lead us from our more familiar patterns of worship, that we might see that God is "worthy" at all times and in all situations.

Occasionally the Enemy will harass us through depression or disappointment and actually exploit our desire for honesty before God. The last thing we want to do is mechanically draw nigh to God with our lips when our hearts (feelings) are seemingly directed otherwise. The Holy Spirit impressed me once that God was both worthy and faithful whether I felt like it or not. Furthermore, He was ready to receive my prayer and worship if I would honestly offer it to Him in faith and obedience, confessing the truth of His Word.

Once we grasp the faithfulness of God's love for us, we won't be afraid to honestly disclose to Him our innermost thoughts and feelings. In the process, we can honestly face ourselves without fear, for we do so within the protection of God's love. We need never again be threatened by any area of our lives—past or present—because there is nothing too great for God's redeeming grace. We can truly walk into every part of our life without fear, when we go hand-in-hand with the Lord.

Jesus declared that knowledge of the truth would set us free (John 8:32). It will also keep us free. He further equated the truth with Himself: "I *am* the truth" (John 14:6). In other words, truth cannot be discovered by hard thinking—it must be revealed! (John 16:13–14). Truth is not a theoretical pursuit, but a personal encounter and experience with the Lord Jesus Christ Himself.

Real Christian education is not the tireless pursuit of truth, but a meaningful unfolding and realization of truth as it has been discovered in Christ. He is the integrating theme which brings every area of existence into true focus; He is the bridge which relates heavenly purpose to earthly experience.

We are all enrolled in the school of the Spirit. It is a personal comfort to know that our Heavenly Teacher is highly qualified. May we be dedicated disciples as He directs us to follow the truth at all times—speaking truly, dealing truly, living truly—and thereby become more and more in every way like the Lord Jesus Himself.

4

HOLY SPIRIT BAPTISM: PART ONE
What Meaneth This?

He said therefore to the multitude . . . "I indeed *baptize* you with (in) water for repentance, but He who is coming after me is mightier than I, whose sandals I am not worthy to carry; He will *baptize* you with (in) the Holy Spirit and with fire." (Matt. 3:7, 11 various versions)

And he preached, saying, "After me comes He who is mightier than I, the thong of whose sandals I am not worthy to stoop down and untie. I have *baptized* you with water, but He will *baptize* you with the Holy Spirit." (Mark 1:7–8 various versions)

John answered them all, "I *baptize* you with water; but He who is mightier than I is coming, the thong of whose sandals I am not worthy to untie; He will *baptize* you with the Holy Spirit and with fire." (Luke 3:16 various versions)

And John bore witness, "I saw the Spirit descend as a dove from heaven, and it remained on Him. I myself did not know Him; but He who sent me to *baptize* with water said to me, 'He on whom you see the Spirit descend and remain, this is He who *baptizes* with the Holy Spirit.' " (John 1:32–33 various versions)

And while staying with them, He (Jesus) charged them not to depart from Jerusalem, but to wait for the promise of the Father, which, He said, you heard from me, for John *baptized* with water, but before many days you shall be *baptized* with the Holy Spirit. (Acts 1:4–5 various versions)

And I (Peter) remembered the word of the Lord, how He said, "John baptized with water, but you shall be baptized with the Holy Spirit." (Acts 11:16 various versions)

UTILIZATION OF THE WORD BAPTISM IN GREEK LIFE AND LITERATURE

There are interesting parallels between water baptism and Holy Spirit Baptism which we shall want to consider in some detail. The words "baptize" and "baptism" are derived directly from the corresponding Greek verb, *baptizo* and the noun *baptisma*. The English language has no words of its own with equivalent meaning, therefore the Greek terms were transliterated in anglicized form. To appreciate the full value and feeling these words convey, we must consider their usage in the Greek life and literature of New Testament times.

Baptism: Mechanical Usage

The terms were used in a number of revealing ways. In a mechanical (physical) way, the verb *baptizo* referred to:

1. The dipping of a fabric into a vat of dye with the intent that every fiber of the fabric will take up the quality (color) of the dye and forever after be changed in its character. The effect of this baptism will be apparent for all to see.
2. The plunging of a hot iron (as a sword) into cold water that the tempering process would alter interior molecular arrangement conferring strength and durability. It is a baptism which ensures a hard cutting edge that will maintain its sharpness.
3. The sinking of a ship to the extent it is completely submerged. Not only is the ship in the water, but the water is in the ship. Every recess, corner and compartment is flooded by the baptismal experience. Every inch of the inside and outside surface is exposed to the wetting power of the water.

4. The soaking to saturation of a sponge as it is placed into a liquid. Every space in the sponge will be filled with the baptismal waters. The same thought is expressed by the soaking of food in wine that the flavor of the wine will be conferred upon the food, as an effect of its baptism.
5. The filling-by-dipping process by which water is drawn from a well by a bucket. The baptism of the bucket is the means by which the refreshing qualities of the water in the well are distributed to those who are dry and thirsty.

Baptism: Ceremonial Usage

The verb *baptizo* is also used in regard to certain ceremonial (religious ritual) functions:

1. The washing of cups, pots, and brasen vessels by the Pharisees (Mark 7:4) is a reference to ceremonial cleansing and purification. There are many references in the Septuagint (a third-century B.C. Greek translation of the Old Testament) to *baptizo* as the word relates to ceremonial bathing and washing. One interesting passage concerns the washing and cleansing of Naaman the Leper in the Jordan River (II Kings 5:14).
2. John's baptism was an initiatory rite which played a prominent role in his prophetic ministry of preparing the people for the advent of their Messiah. It publicly signified personal repentance and a commitment to good works (Luke 3:1–16). John's message heralded the coming of a Heavenly King in His dual role of Savior and Baptizer (Matt. 3:1–3; John 1:29,33).

   Jesus submitted to John's baptism as a personal endorsement of John's message and mission. In so doing, He not only identified Himself with sinful humanity, but committed Himself to His role as the "Lamb of God who taketh away the sins of the world." The ministry of Jesus would produce in the lives of John's converts what John's ministry had prepared them for—everlasting life and spiritual power in the Kingdom of God.
3. Christian baptism took over where John's baptism left off. After the cross and following Pentecost, the rite of water baptism took on a dual significance concerning God's life and

power which we shall discuss shortly. The basic thought, however, at this point in our thinking is that we are "introduced" or "placed" into a new sphere of existence—an environment which is alive with God's love, an atmosphere which is heavenly in its character.

The ordinance or sacrament of water baptism also speaks of our being introduced into the beautiful mystery of the Trinity (Matt. 28:19). The name of the Father, Son, and Holy Ghost represents the very nature of the Godhead in terms of divine life, love, and truth—all of which we experience through our relationship with the Lord Jesus. "In him dwelleth all the fulness of the Godhead bodily" (Col. 2:9). This new relationship is one of privilege and responsibility.

Baptism: Metaphorical Usage

There is also a *metaphorical* (analogical) use of *baptizo* in secular literature and Holy Scriptures. Here the thought relates to being overwhelmed, as with joy or sorrow. Jesus used the term when He spoke to His disciples of His forthcoming crucifixion: "I have a baptism to be baptized with; and how I am straitened (constrained, pressed with anguish) until it be accomplished" (Luke 12:50 various versions). The Lord realized He soon would be overwhelmed with suffering, as He would take upon Himself the consequences of our sin.

The verb for "baptize" is also used metaphorically in two other senses in the New Testament. One is in reference to a baptism of fire, which many commentators feel may picture the overwhelming judgment of God upon the Christ-rejecting Jews. Others see in this a reference to the plunging and purifying power of God's Spirit which is to cleanse our lives (Matt. 3:11).

The same passage also speaks of a baptism by Jesus for the believer whereby he is to be flooded and overwhelmed by

God's Spirit: "He [Jesus] shall *baptize* you with the Holy Ghost and with fire."

All of the various shades of meaning and different usages in the Greek for *baptizo* and *baptisma* contribute to our understanding of Holy Spirit Baptism. Many times spiritual experience falls short of its intended purpose because we are not totally aware of what we have—and what has us. Truth cannot be completely translated into life until it has been fully appreciated; only then can it be actualized by a vigorous faith. If our spiritual vision is blurred, our faith will be fuzzy and have little force or direction. It is our intention to consider in detail the purpose and releasing power which Holy Spirit Baptism can bring to our personal experience in Christ.

THREEFOLD FOUNDATION FOR THE CHRISTIAN LIFE

The apostle Peter dramatically describes for us the basic foundation for our life in Christ in the sermon which immediately followed his own Baptism in the Spirit on the Day of Pentecost. In response to the cry of the conscience-stricken crowd, "What shall we do (to be saved)?" Peter instructs them as follows:

Repent, and be baptized [water] every one of you in the name of Jesus Christ for the remission of sins, and ye shall receive the gift of the Holy Ghost. For the promise is unto you, and to your children, and to all that are afar off. (Acts 2:38–39)

Three fundamental blocks in God's great redemptive plan for man's full salvation are laid down: *repentance, baptism,* and *reception* of the Spirit. They can be viewed as different phases of the same foundational work accomplished by our Redeemer, the Lord Jesus Christ. The Scriptures describe each phase as a baptism, unified by the dual role which Christ plays as our Savior and Baptizer. He is the one and only foundation upon which our lives can rest (I Cor. 3:11). The three baptismal phases or stages which are in the foundation for our faith will now be considered in some detail.

First Foundational Phase: Repentance—Baptism into Christ's Body

Repentance (conversion) brings the new believer to his baptism into the Body of Christ:

> You stubborn and stiff-necked people, heathen in heart and ears, you are always actively resisting the Holy Spirit. (Acts 7:51 various versions)

> Repent—change your mind and purpose; turn around and return to God, that your sins may be erased, that times of refreshing—reviving with fresh air—may come from the presence of the Lord. (Acts 3:19 TAB modified)

> For by one Spirit are we all *baptized* into one body . . . and have been all made to drink into one Spirit. (I Cor. 12:13)

> For ye are all the children of God by faith in Christ Jesus. For as many of you as have been *baptized* into Christ have put on Christ. (Gal. 3:26–27)

The *candidate* for Body baptism is the repentant believer; the *baptizer* is the Holy Spirit; and the baptismal *medium* is the living Body of Christ. The Holy Spirit personally convicts us of sin, convinces us we need a Savior, and then introduces to and into the saving life of Christ. In receiving the Lord by faith into our lives, we are all indwelt by His Spirit:

> If anyone does not have the Spirit of Christ, he does not belong to him. . . . But if the Spirit of Him who raised Jesus from the dead dwells in you, He who raised Christ Jesus from the dead will also give life to your mortal bodies through His Spirit who *indwells* you. (Rom. 8:9, 11 NASB)

In other words, the Holy Spirit—as the Spirit of Christ—indwells the new convert with the life and presence of the Lord. At the same time, the new believer is also baptized (introduced) into the Body of Christ where he finds his place among the other members. (In Acts 2:41–47, the community [Body] life of the first charismatic fellowship is fully described. For further discussion, see the chapter entitled "Fellowship in the Spirit" in the author's book, *Overflowing Life*.)

To be baptized into the Body of Christ—which then becomes our new environment for life—is also pictured by Jesus in His discourse concerning the vine and its branches (John 15). It is as we are grafted into Christ (the true vine) that we (the many branches) find our source of life and purpose for living (to bear fruit). As we so abide in the vine (Christ), its life (Holy Spirit) flows through our being, enabling us to mature and become fruitful (spiritual gifts and graces). In conversion, therefore, the Holy Spirit is seen to both baptize (introduce) us into the Body of Christ and indwell us with the Spirit of Christ. He will next want to fill and flood us to *overflowing* as we also appropriate the power of Holy Spirit Baptism (third phase).

Second Foundational Phase: Water Baptism

Water baptism refers to the ordinance or sacrament of Christian baptism as it was commanded by the Lord in His Great Commission:

> Go ye therefore, and teach all nations, baptizing them in the name of the Father and of the Son, and of the Holy Ghost. (Matt. 28:19)

The *candidate* for water baptism is the new believer; the *baptizer* is a qualified disciple; and the *medium* is water. The mode (sprinkling, pouring, immersion) varies with different traditions, but probably was by immersion (where possible) in the early Church, according to historians. The practice was faithfully followed by the early disciples (Acts 8:12; 10:47; 19:4–5).

There is rich and beautiful symbolism in the ceremony of water baptism which relates both to conversion (Body baptism) and to Spirit baptism. First of all, baptismal waters vividly portray for us the *washing of regeneration:*

He saved us not because of any works of righteousness which we have done, but according to His own mercy by the washing (cleansing bath) of *regeneration* (rebirth) and renewing power of the Holy Spirit whom He poured out so richly upon us through Jesus Christ our Saviour. (Titus 3:5–6 various versions)

Secondly, water baptism beautifully represents the *death-burial-resurrection* experience which we share in our union with Christ:

Do you not know that all of us who have been baptized into Christ Jesus have been baptized into His *death?* Therefore we have been *buried* with Him through baptism into death, in order that as Christ was *raised* from the dead through the glory of the Father, so we too might walk in newness of life. For if we have become united with Him in the likeness of His *death,* certainly we shall be also in the likeness of His *resurrection.* (Rom. 6:3–5 NASB, italics mine)

In baptism you were not only *buried* with Him but also *raised* to life with Him because you believed in the power of God who raised Him from the dead. (Col. 2:12 NAB, italics mine)

I am *crucified* with Christ: nevertheless I *live;* yet not I, but Christ liveth in me. (Gal. 2:20)

That [Noah's flood], by the way, is what baptism pictures for us: In baptism we show that we have been saved from death and doom by the *resurrection* of Christ; not because our bodies are washed clean by the water, but because in being baptized we are turning to God and asking him to cleanse our hearts from sin. (I Pet. 3:21 TLB)

Finally, the rite of water baptism is a beautiful prophetic picture of the third foundational phase.

Third Foundational Phase: Holy Spirit Baptism

Receiving the promised gift of the Holy Spirit for power (Holy Spirit Baptism) naturally follows our discussion of water baptism, for the latter vividly pictures this third and last phase of Christ's redemptive work. The *candidate* for Spirit Baptism is the recently water-baptized believer. (God can reverse His order, and occasionally individuals are baptized in the Spirit before being baptized in water [Acts 10:44–48].) The *baptizer* is the Lord Jesus Christ. The baptismal *medium* is the presence of the Holy Spirit which streams forth from the throne of God:

I (John) have baptized you with water, but He (Jesus) will baptize you in the Holy Spirit. (Mark 1:8 various versions)

Just as one is flooded by the waters of Christian baptism, so is each life to be flooded by the spiritual power of God's living river of love:

For God's *love* has been poured forth (flooded) into our hearts through the Holy Spirit which has been given to us. (Rom. 5:5 various versions)

But you shall receive *power* when the Holy Spirit has come upon you. (Acts 1:8 NASB)

The purpose of Holy Spirit Baptism is to empower the believer that he may develop and express his new life in Christ Jesus. Both the fruit and the gifts of the Spirit are essential for proper growth and effective ministry.

SCRIPTURAL BASIS FOR THE
THREEFOLD PATTERN

The threefold pattern of repentance-baptism-reception which corresponds to Body, water, and Spirit baptism is repeatedly referred to throughout the Book of Acts:

1. Following Pentecost, some three thousand repentant souls were baptized in water and immediately became actively involved in the newly formed charismatic community (Acts 2:41–47).
2. Philip preached in Samaria following the dispersal from Jerusalem because of persecution. Many repented, were baptized in water and had hands laid upon them that they might receive (be baptized in) the Holy Spirit (Acts 8:5–17).
3. Philip instructed the Ethiopian on the road to Gaza. He was baptized in water following his confession of faith. The powerful presence of the Holy Spirit on this occasion was evidenced by Philip's dramatically being caught away, leaving the Ethiopian filled with joy. Spirit baptism is not directly indicated, but possibly is inferred (Acts 8:26–39).
4. Saul's conversion involves repentance, water baptism, and the infilling (Baptism) with the Holy Spirit (Acts 9:1–19).
5. Peter's witness to the Gentiles in the house of Cornelius resulted in their being converted and receiving the Holy Spirit which was outpoured upon them (Spirit Baptism). They then were allowed to be baptized in water (Acts 10:34–48).
6. Paul's encounter with some of John's disciples in Ephesus, some twenty years after Pentecost, also involved water baptism and the oncoming of the Holy Spirit (Spirit Baptism).

FOUNDATIONAL INTEGRITY

In summary, we can now appreciate that the sacrament or ordinance of water baptism is a *ceremonial* rite which *metaphori-*

cally gathers up and portrays the spiritual meaning related to both Body baptism and Spirit baptism. It outwardly represents what is an inward reality concerning our *life* relationship with Jesus as the Savior, and our *power* relationship with Jesus as the Baptizer. There is a spiritual unity and continuity to all three baptisms which forms one solid foundation for our faith.

The three phases may be somewhat separated in temporal experience, but they are an integral part of God's one great work of grace in Christ Jesus.

The writers of the New Testament epistles fully appreciated the integrity of our Redeemer's foundational work and viewed it as a whole. Paul expresses this with much feeling and deep understanding:

> Endeavor to keep the unity of the Spirit through the tie of peace. We are all parts of one Body, we have the same Spirit, and we have all been called to the same glorious hope. For there is only one Lord, one faith, and one baptism. We all have the same God and father who rules over all, acts through all and indwells all. (Eph. 4:3–6 various versions)

Perhaps we can summarize graphically the thoughts thus far presented in the chart on the following page.

Parenthetic Historical Note

In the study of Church history, we see that the process of initiation into the Christian community gradually evolved into a formalized religious routine:

1. INSTRUCTION from the *Word* was eventually organized into a carefully structured study (catechism).
2. BAPTISM in *water* became a highly significant and essential ceremony (sacrament).
3. LAYING ON OF HANDS and ANOINTING with *oil* for the purpose of receiving the Holy Spirit became a recognized rite of great importance (confirmation).

THE THREEFOLD FOUNDATION FOR THE CHRISTIAN LIFE

	THE LORD JESUS CHRIST		
	SAVIOR (Life)		**BAPTIZER** (Power)
THREEFOLD BAPTISM	REPENTANCE (Body)	BAPTISM (Water)	RECEPTION (Spirit)
CANDIDATE	CONVERT	CONVERT	CONVERT
BAPTIZER	HOLY SPIRIT	DISCIPLE	JESUS CHRIST
MEDIUM	CHRIST'S LIVING BODY	BAPTISMAL WATERS	HOLY SPIRIT'S PRESENCE
S C R I P T U R E **R E F E R E N C E S**	REPENTANCE: Commanded by Jesus Luke 24:46–49 Preached by the Disciples Acts 7:51 Acts 3:19 (See passages below)	BAPTISM: Commissioned by Jesus Matt. 28:19 Practiced by the Disciples (See passages below)	RECEPTION: Charged by Jesus Luke 24:49 Acts 1:4–5 Administered by the Disciples (See passages below)
	PARALLEL PATTERNS: Acts 2:38 Acts 2:40–41 Acts 8:12 Acts 8:35, 37 Acts 9:6 Acts 10:43 Acts 19:4	PARALLEL PATTERNS: Acts 2:38 Acts 2:41 Acts 8:12 Acts 8:36, 38 Acts 9:18 Acts 10:47–48 Acts 19:4–5	PARALLEL PATTERNS: Acts 2:38 Acts 2:43 Acts 8:14–17 Acts 8:39 Acts 9:17 Acts 10:44–47 Acts 19:6
	BODY BAPTISM I Cor. 12:13 Gal. 3:26–27 John 15:5 Eph. 5:23, 30 I Cor. 12:12, 27 Rom. 12:5	WATER BAPTISM Acts 22:16 Titus 3:5–6 I Pet. 3:21 Rom. 6:3–5 Col. 2:12 Mark 1:8 John 1:33–34	SPIRIT BAPTISM Matt. 3:11 Mark 1:7–8 Luke 3:16 John 1:32–34 Acts 1:5 Acts 11:16
	CHRIST'S BIRTH Matt. 1:18 Luke 1:26–27, 35 II Cor. 5:21 I John 3:5	CHRIST'S BAPTISM Matt. 3:13–15 Mark 1:9 Luke 3:21	CHRIST'S ANOINTING Luke 3:22; 4:1, 14, 18 John 3:34 Acts 10:38 Col. 1:19; 2:9
	INDWELLING LIFE John 4:10–14 John 7:37–38 Rom. 8:9–11 I John 5:11–12 Rev. 22:17	SPIRITUAL POWER Luke 24:49 Acts 1:8 Acts 4:33 Rom. 15:13 Rom. 15:19 Eph. 3:16	OVERFLOWING LIFE John 7:37–38 Acts 2:4 Acts 4:31 Acts 6:3, 5, 8 Acts 13:52 Rom. 15:13 Eph. 5:18–20

4. FELLOWSHIP around the *bread* and *wine* of the Lord's table developed into an elaborate but very solemn celebration (Eucharist).

There was purpose and rich beauty in the religious forms so established, and there is safety in divine order and authority when motivated by God's Spirit. Structure without Spirit, however, is powerless to set people free from their bondages or heal the pain within their hearts. How often people have routinely gone to church year in and year out without truly being helped where they hurt. How very much we need to return to the healing streams which can revive and release our lives for God's glorious end-time purpose—a people radiant with His life and love.

VICTORY THROUGH SURRENDER

Having established a background concerning the foundation for our faith, we will now consider in detail the significance of Holy Spirit Baptism in terms of our own inner needs for healing and deliverance.

I recall someone expressing concern that in our emphasis on the blessing of Spirit Baptism we depreciate the need for the work of the cross in our lives. It is true we must never under-estimate the essential and central place of the cross, for it is the only gateway to our life in God. It speaks of submission and surrender as the keys to victory. Jesus established the principle and fulfilled the pattern: He was totally submissive to the will of His Father, and completely yielded to the power of the Holy Spirit. As his death brought life—resurrection life—so will ours.

To imply, however, that the Baptism in the Holy Spirit is somehow apart from the principle of the cross, is to have a limited understanding of all that is divinely involved in the experience. We humbly approach the Baptizer with a heart attitude of faith, love, and obedience, ready to submit and entrust our lives to His care. Our intent is that He place us into the stream of the Spirit—God's overflowing river of love, truth, and power. Henceforth our desire is to be led of the Spirit and thereby assume the privileges and responsibilities of sonship (Rom. 8:14). Fulfillment of God's goal for our lives is determined by the extent to which we daily remain surrendered to His Holy Spirit. The cross is central in Holy Spirit Baptism. A woman once pointed this out to me in regard to the word itself—bap†ism!

Yes, death is the doorway to life:

> Whosoever will save his life shall lose it; and whosoever will lose his life for my sake shall find it. . . . If any man will come after me, let him deny himself, and take up his cross, and follow me. . . . I am the way, the truth and the life . . . I am come that they might have life, and that they might have it more abundantly! (Matt. 16:25, 24; John 10:10)

The enemy presents to us a distorted concept of the cross that implies that its work in our lives will leave us impoverished in our personhood. Our daily walk will be reduced to a cold, limited, colorless, hollow experience. Anything that brings joy or pleasure will automatically be evil. The cross-life is equated with a grim, gray, grit-your-teeth-grin-and-bear-it existence. Actually, such a perverted attitude is one of the first things that needs the work of the cross. We should be dead to Satan's slander concerning the love and wisdom of God. The Lord didn't come to eliminate us—but to set us free.

Freedom comes, however, as we learn to surrender ourselves to the sovereignty of God's Spirit. He understands us far better than we understand ourselves and knows how in God's will our lives can be filled with His love, joy, and peace. There is divine purpose and destiny in our selfhood which only the Holy Spirit can realize. If we try to "save" (know, find, express) ourselves by ourselves, we will actually lose our lives as far as eternal and spiritual values are concerned. Man has been born with eternity in his heart and cannot be truly satisfied in his spirit without a heavenly perspective (Eccles. 3:11 TAB). Earthly achievement and recognition can bring a transitory sense of satisfaction, but something within us cries out for the meaning which only eternal life in Christ Jesus can bring.

We cannot *be* ourselves, *by* ourselves—which is why God has sent us His Spirit. He alone can make our individual worlds worthwhile, if we will yield to Him that privilege. He gives us not only the power to *live,* but also to *die* (Rom. 8:13). We will never get to the cross, let alone stay there, apart from His help. We just don't have the lifting-power in ourselves to get our cross on the roadway to life to which Jesus has called us. No wonder the Holy Spirit is called "the paraclete" (one who stands by to strengthen).

By God's grace and the power of His Spirit, the cross truly becomes a gateway to abundant life. Through that door we enter into the realm of the Spirit. This is not some spooky, mystical experience which disconnects us from our earthly existence, but rather a relationship with the Holy Spirit which allows us to be a whole person for His glory—as Jesus was. The cross does not lead to a realm of fear and frustration, but to joy, peace, and freedom.

Like a River Glorious

As a boy, I enjoyed swimming in a mountain stream in the back country of Southern Washington. In one place the river was rather deep and swift, but it eventually broadened out downstream into a wide shallow area suitable for wading. It was most exhilarating to plunge into the rushing water upstream and be swept along under the control and power of the river until the shallow portion was reached, where once again one could navigate by foot to the stream-side.

It is a little strange that one would find such joy in a medium which does not allow the same control of locomotion as two feet pulled to the ground by gravity. Once in the river, a person gave up the regulation of his direction, and the movement of the water became the controlling agent. Why would anyone want to forfeit the freedom that is found in walking about on the earth?

The answer is found in the new order of freedom which the buoyancy of running water provides. The lifting, carrying power of the river enables one to exercise a degree of movement utterly impossible while he is grounded. A person can turn somersaults, fly like a bird, and gracefully execute many other maneuvers which are ordinarily completely prohibited by the earthly pull of gravity.

I experienced a similar sense of elation during my first skin-diving venture off the Southern California coast. After learning how to breathe through a snorkel, and maneuver out beyond the breakers, I discovered a whole new underwater world. Waving fields of sea-grass, rocky outcroppings studded with brightly colored starfish and sea urchins, brilliant orange-colored fish swimming gracefully along in the sunlit seawater —here was a realm of existence which previously had been known to me only in a secondhand, textbook sort of way. It took a "baptism" in the ocean before I could discover the secrets of the sea.

I expressed some of these thoughts at a Catholic retreat house some time ago. Afterward, one of the sisters approached me and shared some beautiful experiences related to her work as a physical therapist. One involved a little girl crippled from birth so seriously that little movement was possible to her without mechanical support. Her first visit to the hydrotherapy pool was like witnessing a miracle in the making. As the little child relaxed and yielded to the buoyancy of the warm water, she discovered even her weakened muscles were capable of producing body movements never before experienced. With cries of joy and gladness, she exclaimed over and over again, "Look, I can hop and skip like other little girls—I can even jump and dance!" She had found a new realm of freedom, and with it a whole new way of life.

An elderly man in the same hospital became a helpless and hopeless cripple confined to his bed and chair. In bitter sadness, he withdrew from all social contacts and spent his time alone watching television. One day the therapist finally persuaded him to try the therapy pool. To his amazement, he discovered he could float on his back and propel himself all over the pool with his feet. The soft but sure support of the water permitted weakened limbs to function in ways otherwise impossible. Furthermore, when some children entered the water with him, he immediately began to instruct them in enjoying freedom of movement. He shared with an enthusiasm that only personal experience could bring.

It is hardly necessary to make the spiritual application: those who are crippled in soul and spirit already have felt the longing in their hearts to be lifted beyond their own limitations into the liberty which is promised by God's Spirit (II Cor. 3:17). The parallel between water baptism and Spirit Baptism now becomes unusually clear: just as the *outer* man gets wet all over in water baptism; so is the *inner* man to get wet all over in Spirit Baptism. Every fiber in the fabric of our inner being is to be changed for God's glory. No nook, cranny, or recess of our soul is to be unreached by the surging, searching streams of God's life-giving Spirit. The hidden person of the heart is to be adorned with the beauty and charm of a gentle and peaceful spirit which is neither anxious or wrought up (I Pet. 3:4 TAB).

O Lord my God, I cried to You and You have healed me. . . . You have turned my mourning into dancing for me; You have put off my sackcloth and girded me with gladness, To the end that my tongue and my heart and *everything glorious within me* may sing praise to You, and not be silent. O Lord my God, I will give thanks to You for ever. (Ps. 30:2, 11–12 TAB, italics mine)

5

~≋ HOLY SPIRIT BAPTISM: PART TWO

Immersion of the Inner Man

May the God of peace (divine harmony) Himself sanctify (hallow, purify, consecrate) you wholly (through and through, completely); and I pray God your whole (entire) *spirit, soul* and *body* be preserved blameless (sound, faultless) at the coming of our Lord Jesus Christ. Faithful is He who is calling you for He will do it—sanctify and preserve you completely. (I Thess. 5:23–24 various versions)

THE TRIPARTITE NATURE OF MAN

To understand the full significance of Spirit Baptism, we must appreciate the functions and qualities of the inner man. Only the Maker of man fully understands the makeup of man; only He can refresh the spirit, re-fashion the soul, and shape our lives into the image of His Son. The life of Jesus Christ is our example of the totally integrated personality—spirit, soul, and body. He possessed an inner harmony of heart and mind which enabled Him to become for us the living and personal expression of God's love and truth. He is our pattern for perfect manhood—life as God intended man to live it—forever!

Baptism portrays for us a life that is to be totally touched by the perfecting and releasing power of God's love. The inner man is indeed to get washed all over in the healing stream of His Holy Spirit. This divine concept of completeness and inner harmony enables us to relate the heavenly and earthly aspects of our daily lives.

There are quantitative (wholeness) and qualitative (faultless) aspects in the Scripture passage above. God desires that not one part of our makeup be untouched by the *perfecting* and *preserving* power of His Spirit. Man is described as being composed of three interrelated and interdependent parts: spirit, soul and, body—*pneuma, psuche,* and *soma* in the Greek.

The Bible sometimes uses the terms "spirit" and "soul" synonymously, but at other times seems to differentiate between the two. We are informed in Hebrews 4:12, that God's Word can divide man's soul from his spirit. In our study it is the unique qualities of spiritual and soulish functions with which we are interested. We want to understand how the Holy Spirit desires to influence our life within. We are warned not to be ignorant of the devil's devices in his oppressive activities (in the heart and mind) toward the saints (II Cor. 2:11). For these reasons, we wish to become better acquainted with ourselves—spirit, soul, and body—that we might more meaningfully submit to God's Spirit and effectively resist the devil (James 4:7).

RELATED LEVELS OF LIFE

Man was created to live. Three interrelated levels of life are recognized in Scripture; man's divine destiny involves all three. First, there is the realm of *biological* or organic life defined by the Greek word *bios.* It is from this term that our word "biology" (*bios* + *logos*) is derived. Biology is the science of life as it pertains to our natural world. In this sense, "biotic" life relates to the *body* of man.

Secondly, there is the realm of *psychological* or conscious life of the individual which is associated with the Greek word *psuche*. Psychology (*psuche* + *logos*) is the science of the mind. The word "soul" is derived from the same term (*psuche*), so one could view psychology as the study of the soul. Psychic life, as so defined, relates to the *soul* of man.

Finally, there is the realm of *spiritual* life, which involves the divine qualities of eternal life. The Greek term for spiritual life is *zoe*. The word "quicken" (*zoopoieo*) means literally "make alive," and refers to our life in the Spirit. "Zoetic" life properly relates to the *spirit* of man.

The chart on the following page will be helpful in our subsequent discussion.

Obviously, spiritual truth cannot be completely compressed into man-made charts or schemes. However, behind such necessary frames of reference is reality, and this is what we seek to find; then we shall trust God's Spirit to translate that truth into life.

The Spirit of Man

The spirit (*pneuma*) of man, apart from the ministry of the Holy Spirit, is lifeless (insensitive) to the spiritual, heavenly, and eternal (zoetic) realm. This is the condition of those who are dead in trespasses and sin (Eph. 2:1-3). For this reason Jesus said we must be born again (John 3:1-13). In the new-birth experience, our spirits are quickened (made alive) by God's Spirit (Ezek. 36:26-28). "He that is *joined* unto the Lord is *one* spirit!" (I Cor 6:17, italics mine). Two-dimensional (soul-body) existence now includes a third dimension: that of the spirit. In other words, we have been lifted from the psychic-biotic level of life to the zoetic (eternal life) level. Full

THE TRIPARTITE BEING OF MAN

	SPIRIT–*PNEUMA* INNERMOST BEING	SOUL–*PSUCHE* MIND AND HEART	BODY–*SOMA* FLESH AND BLOOD
SPHERE OF AWARENESS	GOD (1)	SELF (1)	WORLD (1)
LEVEL OF LIFE	SPIRITUAL (ZOETIC) (1)	PSYCHOLOGICAL (PSYCHIC) (1)	BIOLOGICAL (BIOTIC) (1)
REALM OF ACTIVITY	SUPERNATURAL (1)	MENTAL (1)	PHYSICAL (1)
RELATED DIMENSIONS	HEAVENLY ETERNAL (1)	EARTHLY TEMPORAL (1)	EARTHLY TEMPORAL (1)
BENEFITS OF SALVATION	JUSTIFICATION (ONCE AND FOR ALL) PENALTY OF SIN (2)	SANCTIFICATION (DAILY) POWER OF SIN (2)	GLORIFICATION (AT CHRIST'S RETURN) PRESENCE OF SIN (2)
PARTICULAR RELATIONSHIP TO GOD	IN OUR SPIRIT WE STAND AS SONS BEFORE THE FATHER (POSITION) (3)	IN OUR SOUL WE INCREASE IN CHRIST'S LIKENESS (PROGRESSION) (3)	IN OUR BODY WE HOUSE AND HONOR THE HOLY SPIRIT (POSSESSION) (3)
CORRESPONDING SCRIPTURE REFERENCES	(1) John 4:23–24 I Cor. 2:11–14 I Cor. 15:45–53 II Cor. 4:18 Eph. 2:4–7	(1) Psalm 13:2 Psalm 42:2, 4–5 I Cor. 2:13–16 II Cor. 4:18 I John 2:17	(1) Num. 13:27–33 Matt. 14:14 John 3:6 I Cor. 15:50 II Cor. 4:18
	(2) Rom. 3:24, 28 Titus 3:7	(2) Luke 9:23 I Cor. 15:31 II Cor. 3:18 Gal. 5:16 Phil. 2:12–13	(2) I Cor. 15:44–54 Phil. 3:21
	(3) John 1:12 Gal. 4:6	(3) II Cor. 3:18 I Pet. 2:2 II Pet. 3:18	(3) I Cor. 3:16 I Cor. 6:19–20

spiritual potential is developed as our quickened (life) spirits are further energized (power) by our Baptism in the Holy Spirit.

Man's spirit when quickened and energized by God's Spirit can receive divine revelation, respond in prayer and worship, and enter into communion with God. The spirit of man engages in spiritual witness and warfare, and becomes the faculty for spiritual discernment; it also shares in the fellowship of the saints.

The inner senses of the spirit now become active, and eternal and heavenly realities can be perceived. Man's spirit also becomes the ground from which the fruit of the Spirit is grown, and is the receiving area for the spiritual gifts. All of these functions are necessary before our destiny in Christ Jesus can be fulfilled. A two-dimensional man is a seriously deficient individual in God's sight. The three-dimensional man is His continuing joy and delight.

The Soul of Man

Man's soul (*psuche*) is the seat of his personality and selfhood: The functions of soul establish his identity as a *rational* (mind), *affectionate* (heart) individual. These functions, however, are limited to the boundaries of the mental realm: the realities of heaven and the reaches of eternity are nowhere within touching distance. It takes the power of God's Spirit to break the time barrier and lift man beyond the limitations of earthly attractions. Divorced from the releasing power of the Holy Spirit, man is a mind-bound, time-bound, earthbound, two-dimensional creature—falling far short of the freedom for which he was originally created. Only as his spirit is set free, can the full potential of his soul (personality) be realized.

The soul of man relates to the temporal, earthly, and natural (physical) conditions of life. It is the fountainhead of reason, emotion, volition, memory, imagination, conscience, curiosity, and perception of sensory stimuli. Apart from the control of the Holy Spirit, interacting with and through man's spirit, the soulish functions of man cannot apprehend, express, or relate to heavenly purpose. The soul is geared to the spirit of this world, and becomes the ground upon which the Enemy opposes the things of God. Soulish functions, separated from the life and power of God's Holy Spirit, produce character and conduct described in the Scriptures under such terms as fleshly, carnal, unregenerate, and natural (Rom. 8; I Cor. 2; Gal 5 TAB).

The Body of Man

Man has a body (*soma*) by which he relates to and interacts with the natural world around him. He senses out the character of his living and non-living environment and responds either reflexively or reflectively in what is usually a life-promoting fashion. He may adjust himself to his world, or his world to himself. (We can move away from the heater or turn the thermostat down.) He can also express to the world behavior which spontaneously springs from within without prior prompting by sensory stimuli. In other words, the expression may not be a direct response to circumstances, but may be based on inspiration (good or evil) from within. Reflex (automatic, involuntary) responses may be *unlearned* (unconditioned), such as the pain reflex or the knee-jerk reflex. There are also *learned* (conditioned) responses such as that illustrated by Pavlov's dog. Feeding stimulates reflex salivary secretion. Pavlov discovered by repeatedly ringing a bell at each feeding, the dog eventually would salivate by the bell whether food was present or not. He had produced a learned or conditioned reflex. (The devil is a great bell-ringer!)

We can summarize the presentation thus far by the following outline:

FUNCTIONS: SPIRIT–SOUL–BODY

I. SPIRIT (PNEUMA)
  A. Revelation from God (I Cor. 2:10)
    1. Illumination: inspired understanding of God's Word
    2. Intuition: divine insight apart from reason
    3. Instruction: inspired counsel and instruction from another teacher or prophet of God
    4. Observation: recognition of divine purpose in natural circumstances
  B. Prayer to God (Eph. 6:18)
    1. Confession: agreement with God concerning *our* sin and *His* Son
    2. Petition: presentation of our needs
    3. Intercession: pleading on the behalf of others
    4. Praise: worship in spirit and in truth
  C. Communion with God (II Cor. 13:14)
    1. Awareness: inner witness of His abiding presence
    2. Attitude: expectant orientation toward the "open" heavens
  D. Witness to man (Ministry) (Acts 1:8)
    1. Words: truth in love
    2. Deeds: love in action
    3. Appearance: portrait of Christ
  E. Discernment of spirits (I Cor. 12:10)
    1. From God: Holy Spirit
    2. From Man: human spirit
    3. From Satan: evil spirit
  F. Fellowship with man (I Cor. 12:12–13, I John 1:3)
    1. Worship: praising God together
    2. Word: studying God's truth together
    3. Witness: sharing God's life together
    4. Work: serving the Lord together
    5. Warfare: opposing the enemy together
  G. Warfare with Satan (Eph. 6:12)
    1. Weapons: Spirit and the Word
    2. Authority: divine commission
    3. Power: blood of Christ

    4. Standard: cross of Jesus

H. Spiritual (inner) senses (Heb. 5:14)
    1. Vision
    2. Hearing
    3. Taste
    4. Smell
    5. Touch-Temperature
    6. Balance
    (Note: The spiritual senses contribute to the functions listed above)

I. Seedbed for spiritual fruit (Gal. 5:22–23)
    1. Sown in the Spirit
    2. Fruition in the soul
    3. Expressed through the body
        a. Love
        b. Joy
        c. Peace
        d. Long-suffering
        e. Gentleness
        f. Goodness
        g. Faithfulness
        h. Meekness
        i. Temperance

J. Receiving department for spiritual gifts (I Cor. 12:8–10)
    1. Received in the spirit
    2. Registered in the soul
    3. Administered through the body (word and/or deed)
        a. Wisdom
        b. Knowledge
        c. Discernment
        d. Prophecy
        e. Tongues
        f. Interpretation
        g. Faith
        h. Miracles
        i. Healings

II. SOUL (PSUCHE)
   A. Reason: think (meditation, conception)
   B. Emotion: feel (passion, affection)
   C. Volition: will (decision)
   D. Memory: recall (remembrance-reflection)
   E. Imagination: create (envision, dream)
   F. Conscience: judge (discernment)
   G. Curiosity: inquire (exploration)
   H. Perception: interpret (sensation-cognition)

III. BODY (SOMA)
   A. Reception: sense information
   B. Reaction: motor responses (words/deed)
      1. Reflexive (automatic-involuntary)
         a. Learned: conditioned
         b. Unlearned: unconditioned
      2. Reflective (deliberate-voluntary)
   C. Expression: motor responses (words/deeds)
      1. Spontaneous (springs from within without prior sensory stimulation)
         a. Soulish source: mind of man
         b. Spiritual source: mind of God or Satan

   All three aspects of man's being—spirit, soul, body—are inter-related and integrated by design into a meaningful whole. Man lives in a body, but he is more than a body. He has a soul, but is more than a soul. He is also a spiritual being. When our spirit is alive and submissive to God's Spirit, the soul is inspired to uniquely express the life of Jesus through our physical body to the world without. *In this way, through man, the earthly things of time and nature are related to God's heavenly, spiritual, and eternal purposes.*

SPIRIT—SOUL—BODY
INTERRELATIONSHIPS

The interrelationships of the spirit, soul, and body can be diagramed in a variety of ways, each emphasizing different aspects of the truth.

The trinity of man can be symbolized as a triangle in which the spirit dominates the lower functions of the body and soul. The unity of man's makeup is properly emphasized. Man must be viewed as a whole, for all of his functions are interrelated, and do not operate as isolated identities.

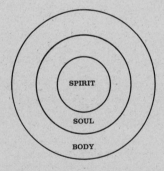

A series of concentric circles convey the centrality of the spirit, man's innermost being. Man's spirit is expressed to and through the soul, which in turn manifests itself through the body to the world without.

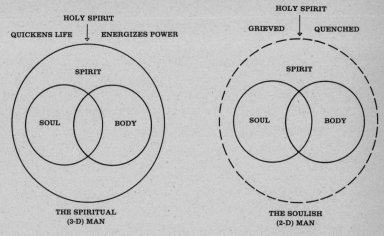

The diagram on the left above illustrates how soulish-physical functions are to be possessed and controlled by the quickened, energized spirit of man. This is truly living in the third dimension (3-D); if the Spirit is quenched, we are reduced to a two-dimensional (2-D) level of existence (right-hand diagram). The Scriptures refer to this as the carnal (fleshly) realm.

Equal, overlapping circles represent the mutual interrelationships of a balanced Christian. Each complete circle is dependent upon the others for full expression of the whole. If any of the respective areas (spirit-soul-body) are under-developed, a lopsided person is the result. The Holy Spirit desires a symmetry in our lives for God's glory and our fulfillment.

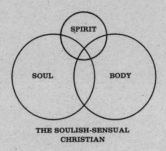

**THE SOULISH-SENSUAL
CHRISTIAN**

The soulish-sensual Christian is the *carnal, fleshly* (2-D) individual who still lives primarily according to his lower, non-spiritual nature. He will be saved but "as by fire" (I Cor. 3:15). Soulish ambition drives him to obtaining a place of earthly power, prestige, and pleasure. When denied, he becomes frustrated and depressed. In either case, he is not much of a witness to the world, for there is little spiritual fruit to be seen. The shy introvert can likewise fall into this category, for attention is still focused on self, in the direction of *avoiding* pain, humiliation, and embarrassment. The result is much the same, spiritually speaking; but God has a gracious answer by His Spirit for both kinds of problems.

The mystically minded Christian is seemingly so preoccu-

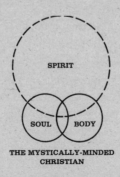

**THE MYSTICALLY-MINDED
CHRISTIAN**

pied with heavenly things he is of no earthly use in fulfilling God's divine purpose in this world. The spirit circle is dotted, for I am not sure but what *true* heavenly minded people will always be of earthly use. Perhaps what we are really talking about are those who have a pseudo-spirituality and use religious experience as an excuse to avoid earthly responsibility.

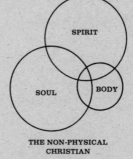

THE NON-PHYSICAL
CHRISTIAN

The non-physical Christian has little care or concern about his body being the temple of the Holy Spirit. Proper diet, rest, and exercise are not seen as spiritual disciplines, but as issues too earthly to command holy attention. Such individuals may either burn out or play out before God's time. Sometimes spiritual and psychological problems have a significant physical basis. A healthy body helps protect the physical side of our soul just as a healthy spirit protects the spiritual side. The Enemy knows we are most vulnerable when we are sick and tired!

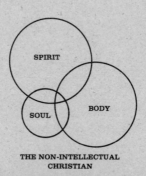

THE NON-INTELLECTUAL
CHRISTIAN

The non-intellectual Christian has great zeal, but little wisdom. He is characterized by having power without purpose. There is much activity, but little is accomplished that is lasting. He would rather watch (and perform) miracles than study truth and walk in disciplined obedience. Because of an unbalanced development, he will limp his way through life, thinking he is at a dead-run for God.

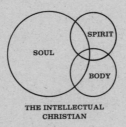

THE INTELLECTUAL
CHRISTIAN

God places no premium on ignorance, but an exalted intellect which is not subservient to the Spirit rebels at the call for discipleship. The Lordship of Jesus Christ is an offensive issue to the intellectual Christian, for it challenges the throne of his natural reason. It is humbling to submit our minds to the mind of Christ, but it is the only way our intellect can realize its full potential in eternal purpose. The tree of knowledge is still growing—and its fruit is still as deadly as ever.

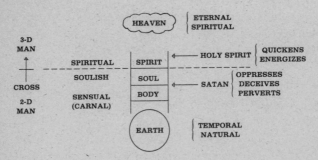

In the above diagram, it is seen that man's spirit when quickened and energized by God's Spirit is open and relates to that which is *heavenly, eternal,* and *spiritual.* His body is exposed to and interacts with that which is *earthly, temporal,* and *natural.* Spiritual reality is registered in the soul at the levels of our understanding and feeling. Appropriate expression to the world is achieved through the body.

Satan seeks to deceive us into living a limited, soulish-sensual (self-centered) life, whereby heavenly purpose is perverted, and God's will through us for earth is frustrated. Furthermore, we are open to oppression and delusion, apart from spiritual defenses.

The cross is set at the boundary of the soul and spirit and becomes the gateway into three-dimensional (3-D) living. God's Word and the Holy Spirit enable us to discern between that which is *soulish* and *spiritual*; and give us the power to die out to the former and become victoriously alive to the latter!

The apostle Paul sums up our thinking with these inspired words:

> To be carnally minded (which is sense and reason without the Holy Spirit) is death—all the miseries arising from sin, both here and hereafter. But to be spiritually minded is life and soul-peace both now and forever. . . . Those who follow the flesh (lower, earthly, sensual, physical nature), mind (pursue and think about) the things of the flesh. . . . If you do live after the flesh you shall die; but if by the power of the Holy Spirit you persistently put to death (crucify) the deeds (sensual pursuits) of the body, you will live life as it really should be lived. (Rom. 8:6, 5, 13 various versions)

PETER: A LIVING EXAMPLE

The contrast between soulish and spiritual responses is vividly pictured for us on one occasion in the life of Peter

(Matt. 16:13–18). Jesus had inquired of the disciples who they thought He really was: "Whom say ye that I am?" Peter immediately and emphatically exclaimed, "Thou art the Christ, the Son of the living God!" With much approval and deep satisfaction, Jesus replied, "Blessed art thou, Simon Bar-jonah [son of an earthly father], for flesh and blood has not revealed it unto thee, but my Father which is in heaven." Here was a revelation of God's Spirit to Peter's spirit. It then registered in his heart and mind, and he confessed it with his mouth. Paul interprets the principle in this way:

> We set forth these truths in words not taught by human wisdom, but by the Holy Spirit. . . . The natural, nonspiritual man does not receive into his heart the revelations of the Holy Spirit, for they don't make any sense to him—they are spiritually discerned. (I Cor. 2:13–14 various versions)

In Matthew, we are startled by an incident which is in sharp contrast to Peter's initial confession. Jesus was informing the disciples that it would be necessary for him to undergo suffering and death at the hands of the elders, priests, and scribes in Jerusalem. Peter sharply reproved Jesus: "God forbid, Lord! This must never happen to You!" (Matt. 16:22 TAB). The Lord's response is most revealing: He turned away from Peter (the rock) and exclaimed, "Out of my way, Satan, for you are a stumbling-stone in my path! Your thoughts are not God's thoughts, but those of men" (Matt. 16:23 various versions).

What is the explanation behind this conversion of a building-block into a stumbling-stone? Jesus provided the answer: Peter's mind, not controlled by God's Spirit as before, actually became the ground for Satanic temptation—"Peter, you are speaking as from the mind of man; not from the mind of God." In other words, in a *soulish* way, Peter was speaking from the top of his head, and the bottom of his heart. It did not seem *reasonable* to substitute a cross for a crown, when the Kingdom was so close at hand. Furthermore, in a *sentimental* way, it pained Peter to even think someone he loved as much as he loved Jesus should have to suffer. Peter's response was very natural, but also very soulish. It is interesting to observe how Peter's attitude, conversation, and conduct changed after Pentecost. So can ours.

SOULISH FUNCTIONS

Having established some basic principles and a frame of reference regarding the makeup of man, let us consider some practical and personal applications.

Holy Spirit Baptism enhances the operation of the spiritual gifts in the life of the believer. Coupled with God's Word, the gifts of the Spirit enable the Christian to discern between the soul and spirit, and resist Satan's influence toward non-spiritual attitudes and behavior. He is a master psychologist and endeavors to reduce our lives to the soulish level without our being aware of it. We will never crucify the flesh or resist the devil if we don't think this is the source of our problem.

We will now consider the various functions of the soul and some of the difficulties which arise when they are not subservient to the divinely enlightened and energized spirit of man.

Volition

Man was created in God's image, which indicates among other things a sovereignty in his selfhood. The Lord will not violate man's freedom, but invites him to submit his will to God's wisdom whereby the potential of his personality can be divinely fulfilled. Jesus, the perfect pattern for man, has set the example by this life-directing theme: "Not my will but Thine be done!" Man is tempted, however, to ignore God and make his own decisions based on a combination of *reason* and *emotion.*

In regard to their decisions, some individuals are cold and calculating. They carefully analyze and logically reason their way to every conclusion. Their reason-emotion scale would read like this:

```
            3   2   1   0   1   2   3
REASON      |___|___|___|___|___|___|      EMOTION
              ↑          INDICATOR
```

Others are ruled primarily by their emotions:

```
            3   2   1   0   1   2   3
REASON      |___|___|___|___|___|___|      EMOTION
            INDICATOR              ↑
```

We might assume the ideal would be a balanced meter:

```
            3   2   1   0   1   2   3
REASON      |___|___|___|___|___|___|      EMOTION
                      ↑  INDICATOR
```

Apart from God's Spirit, however, both our reason and our emotions can deceive us into making wrong decisions. Peter's endeavor to keep Jesus from the cross is a good example: Both his *head* and *heart* were wrong.

Reason

Satan's motto—"My will not thine be done"—clearly defines the basic root of sin. It was with this disease that he approached man in the very beginning. He succeeded in infecting Adam with the germ of rebellion, and the human race has suffered from a sickness of soul and spirit ever since (Rom. 5:12; I Cor. 15:21–22).

How often we have been tempted to think something through ourselves without first submitting to God's Spirit or consulting His Word. We have the privilege and responsibility of reasoning together with God, yet we so readily rely upon our own wisdom. It is an old story which can be traced all the way back to the Garden of Eden. Two trees were planted by God in the garden: one was the tree of life, and the other was the forbidden tree of knowledge (which when eaten promised death). Hidden in the mystery of the tree of life is Christ Himself—the living way to truth and love. Hidden in the mystery of the tree of knowledge is Satan's alternative—a downward path to error, evil, and death.

Satan approached man at the level of his heart and mind, for the tree spoke of *pleasure* and *wisdom*—apart from God. The Lord's integrity, love, and wisdom were subtly brought into question, and man was tempted to center truth in himself and thereby assume the mastery of his own life. He would determine what was good and evil for himself. By virtue of his knowledge, he would set the course for his own self-realization. An all-too-familiar pattern was established: deception, doubt, disobedience and death. Yes, "There is a way which seemeth right unto [the mind of] a man, but the end thereof are the ways of death" (Prov. 14:12).

The two trees are still growing and can be recognized in the garden of our daily lives. The spirit of truth beckons us to find our life in Christ. To know Him, love Him, serve Him, and pattern our lives after His likeness is the very purpose for our existence—He truly is the Tree of Life. The necessity of submitting our soul to God (the theme of Baptism) in order to realize our destiny is particularly offensive to the intellect of man. Even after conversion and Spirit Baptism, we still have a tendency to help the Lord out with our ideas before *referring* to His Word and *submitting* to His Spirit.

Recognizing counsel from the Body of Christ speaks of Baptism, too, for into that Body we were safely placed in God's will. In one sense, there is no place for the independent thinker in God's economy. There is great need, however, for the dependent thinker—the man who wants his mind sharpened by God's Spirit, honed to a keen edge by His Word, that he might *bless* the Body of Christ.

Jesus is our example. He was the most dependent man who ever lived. In perfect submission to the Holy Spirit, He fulfilled the will of His Father by speaking *His* words and doing *His* deeds. In the process, the uniqueness of His personality was perfectly fulfilled. He found Himself by losing Himself in the will of the Father. So will we.

When the mind is not controlled by God's Spirit, it becomes the ground in which Satan can sow his seeds of thought. A weed-patch of clever, but lifeless, ideas can follow. At other times, deep-rooted doubts and barbed tangles of confusion take over the whole realm of reason.

Emotion

Our feelings are powerful motivating forces which are patterned after the passions of God Himself. They are designed to enable our hearts to beat as one with His. This affinity in affection which enables us to experience and express the *compassion* of the Lord is possible only when our passions are controlled by His Holy Spirit. Otherwise, we will be moved most capriciously by every whim and fancy of our feelings. God wants to harness our hearts, that the energies of affection will be divinely directed for our good and His glory.

These are noble thoughts and lovely words, much easier to write and read on paper than to experience in our lives. We are much too prone to react from soulish passion rather than respond to a situation with spiritual wisdom. Nevertheless, God has given us His Spirit and His Word that we might discern and resist the temptation to be mastered by our emotions. We don't have to think every thought or follow every feeling that arises in our hearts and minds. We are not on the end of the devil's Yo-Yo string, hopelessly and helplessly subjected to his manipulation; we are in the strong, sure hand of God, which can bring a steady sense of direction and purpose to our lives.

Runaway feelings can be triggered by unexpected circumstances, physical, or mental exhaustion, or even Satanic powers which would seek to overwhelm us from without. Dark thoughts and dark feelings reinforce one another, and a self-generating downward spiral of depression can follow. It is at this time the baptizing power of God's Spirit can flood our hearts and minds with light, if we make a decisive move in faith. This is not what we will feel like doing, since the tide of emotion is rushing backward not forward. The Holy Spirit honors right actions, however, _regardless_ of accompanying feelings. How we think or feel is in no way going to alter the faithfulness and worthiness of God; this is the direction our faith is to take. In one sense, doubt is nothing more than misplaced faith.

Faith is characterized by _action_ and _direction_. I have seen my galloping heart reined into control by following a pattern such as this:

1. CONFESS THE LORDSHIP OF JESUS CHRIST and your authority in the Spirit.
2. RESIST THE ENEMY sharply and decisively with God's Word.
3. PRAISE AND WORSHIP GOD _specifically_ for past and present blessings both in the understanding and in the Spirit.
4. DO SOMETHING POSITIVE in faith:
   a. Read God's Word or anything else that is uplifting.
   b. Write a letter, phone or pray for a friend, mow the lawn, or do something else that changes the scene.
   c. Often Spirit-inspired music can calm our inner storms.
   d. Sometimes God wants us to simply rest (physically, mentally, emotionally) in Him.
5. EXPECT A WORD OF WISDOM when God sees we are quiet enough to listen. This may be immediately or when He

sees the timing is right. It may come directly from the Lord, through His Word, from a spiritual counselor, or from a change in circumstances.

We are not to be overwhelmed by our feelings; but rather, *they* are to be baptized into the controlling power of God's Holy Spirit.

Imagination

The imagination is the image-making, pictorial faculty of the mind. The kinds of scenes and portraits pictured on the canvas of our minds is determined by their source: images can be derived from above (divine), within (soulish), or below (Satanic). The pictorial products of our imagination can be all-absorbing. "Some people worship *metal* images; other people worship *mental* images!" In either case, our time, life, and energy is regulated by what we worship or consider worthy of our attention.

The creative abilities of our imagination possess great power for both good and evil. It is not surprising that Satan would seek to either dissipate this power through fantasy and fruitless day-dreaming, or actually usurp it for his own purposes. Most of the references to the imagination in Scripture connect it with the evil conceptions of men which are contrary to the nature and will of God. "And God saw that the wickedness of man was great in the earth, and that every imagination of the thoughts of his heart was only evil continually" (Gen. 6:5).

Our thoughts, feelings, memories, and imaginations mutually influence one another. These functions of the soul provide fertile ground in which the Enemy can sow his seeds of deception. Indeed, he is an exceptionally accomplished artist; but all of his works upon the canvas of our minds are distortions of reality, perverted in perspective. So clever are his presentations, however, that unless we compare them with the real, we can readily be deceived.

The Deceiver is a specialist in portraits—none of which is true to life. He may, for instance, picture God as being so far away, we almost need a telescope to find Him. When we do, we discover He isn't even looking in our direction; or if His face is shown at all, upon His features is painted a frown. Nothing of His love can be seen in any part of the portrait. Satan has other distorted pictures of God as well.

When it comes to his own portrait, Satan will first paint himself completely out of the picture, hoping we will be deceived into thinking he doesn't even exist. A minister-friend once confided in me that he wasn't too sure about the reality of a personal devil. He admitted, however, that he was baffled by a remark his little boy made following a discussion concerning the devil. My friend had carefully explained away Satan's existence as a person and indicated he merely symbolized the influence for evil we find in our world. His boy rather logically replied, "Does that mean, Daddy, that God isn't a person either, but just a kind of influence for good that people like to think about?"

Yes, the Deceiver would like for us to think he is not around, for he knows full well we will never attack (or overcome) an enemy we do not believe exists. Falling short in this tactic, when we recognize from God's Word and experience that Satan is indeed very much alive as a personal, intelligent spirit-being, he will then portray himself with exaggerated dimensions—a huge all-powerful monster, who hides behind every tree, dogs our every step, breathes hot upon our necks, and harasses our entire life.

In the same scene, we are vividly portrayed as helpless, hopeless victims of our villain. One is reminded of the old movie serial, *The Perils of Pauline*, where each episode left the heroine in a precarious position—tied upon the tracks before an oncoming train, unconscious in the path of a vicious buzz saw, or hanging from a ledge by hands weakened by weariness. Dark, dismal pictures are designed to bring and keep us in subjection to Satan's deceiving power.

The Holy Spirit is also a very artistic person, and He specializes in true-life family portraits. We behold God as a Loving Father, who sent His Son that we might find our place in His family. Our Elder Brother is pictured as a meek, sacrificial lamb and a mighty roaring lion; a suffering servant and a triumphant king; a gentle shepherd and a great physician; an all-wise counselor and an almighty deliverer. We also see ourselves as beloved sons and daughters of the King—royal priests with divine powers and privileges. A scepter is in our hand, and words of faith are upon our lips. It is a fearful picture for the Enemy.

Satan does not want us to see who we really are in Christ Jesus—children of God becoming sons of God—strong in the power of His might. Neither does He want us to realize the torment and distress which demon powers experience when Christians confess the Lordship of Jesus. The Lord has sent us in the same power and might with which He was commissioned. Never once was He ever tormented by the powers of evil, rather it was the demonic spirits themselves which cried out in distress when confronted by His presence. This is the illustration which God's Spirit wishes to imprint upon our hearts and vividly picture in our minds.

Improper attitudes can also discolor our imaginations in very soulish ways. I don't know how many times I have engaged in imaginary conversations with people around some matter which I felt was threatening to my principles. "They will say this, and I will say that!" So on goes our little speech within. Even our approach to legitimate issues which must be faced can be spoiled by soulish streaks of pride, jealousy, resentment, and self-pity which mar the lovely image of Jesus in our lives. What we imagine within, we will project without.

Holy Spirit Baptism provides an erasing power by which the

slate of our souls can be cleared of devilish discolorations. The rainbow colors of love, joy, peace, forgiveness, and compassion can then brighten our inner man with God's glory. The Holy Spirit wants not only to erase from our hearts and minds the handiwork of the Enemy, but to restore the beauty of Christ's image therein.

The apostle Paul indicates there is a role that we are to play in the battle for the mind:

> The weapons of our warfare are not carnal (worldly) but mighty (spiritual) through God to the pulling down of strongholds; casting down imaginations (deceptive fantasies) and every high thing (barriers of pride) which exalts itself against the knowledge of God, and bringing into captivity every thought to the obedience (authority) of Christ. (II Cor. 10:4–5 various versions)

This passage clearly indicates that we are not defenseless creatures imprisoned by our thoughts and feelings, but overcomers who have the power and authority to rule our own lives for the glory of God.

Conscience

The conscience is that faculty of the soul that enables man to judge between what is right and wrong, good and evil. It is related to a sense of moral responsibility which, when violated, produces a feeling of guilt. The rule or standard by which the conscience operates can be affected by God, man, and Satan. Paul indicates that all mankind has an inner law or moral instinct which governs their behavior.

> Their own consciences endorse the existence of such a law, for there is something which condemns or excuses their actions. We may be sure that all this will be taken into account in the day of true judgment, when God will judge men's secret lives by Christ Jesus. (Rom. 2:15–16 Phillips)

The conscience is an instrument of the soul which the Holy Spirit can act upon to produce a sense of conviction concerning personal sin and the need for a Savior (John 16:8). God's perfect law is the standard by which men are measured and found wanting. It is used in God's grace to direct us to Jesus that we might be justified by faith (Gal. 3:24). The Holy Spirit acts on man's spirit as a mirror which reveals both God's righteousness (rightness in being and behavior) and man's unrighteousness; man's conscience responds with a sense of guilt which drives him to God's saving grace in Christ Jesus.

The conscience of man is also affected by the society in which he lives. Cultural mores (ethical customs, taboos) are established rules of conduct which regulate behavior within the framework of his social life. His conscience soon conforms to these imposed ethical standards, and guilt is readily experienced whenever a violation occurs. Since such regulations vary from one society to another, a great deal of inner confusion and conflict can occur as one's life enlarges and various social lines are crossed. This is especially true in regard to different religious backgrounds.

Even Christian standards (as interpreted by various groups) differ to a considerable degree. I recall teaching in a Christian college which drew its student body from across the nation. Even within the same denomination there was a real divergence in standards between geographic localities. Rather distinct subcultural differences created some sharp initial reactions on the part of the students.

A similar situation is occurring in the current charismatic renewal. The Holy Spirit is drawing people together around Jesus Christ from a wide variety of religious and cultural backgrounds. It is nothing short of a miracle how traditional and social barriers have been hurdled in the deep desire to worship, learn, witness, and work together in the Lord. Occasionally, however, peripheral differences arise as cultural conformation rather than spiritual reformation is imposed by some upon others. Paul was careful to make allowance for differences in conscience that the possibility of artificially inducing a sense of guilt might be avoided. The Christian's guiding principle is love, not soulish judgment (Rom. 15; I Cor. 10:16–33).

Satan's influence upon the conscience is in the extreme: if he can't sear our conscience, he will endeavor to super-sensitize it. In the first case, the Enemy would seek to insensitize us through willful sin to the convicting and correcting power of the Holy Spirit. To repeatedly grieve the Spirit of God is to ultimately place ourselves beyond His call of grace. The second approach is far more common in the life of the sincere Christian. Satan comes—most convincingly—as the accuser of the brethren and continually keeps the super-sensitive saint under a cloud of condemnation.

I can speak with some conviction concerning the torment of perpetual guilt, for at one time in my life it was an all-too-familiar sickness in my soul. I have discovered, after repeated inquiry, that 60–70 percent of the individuals in most of our meetings have had similar feelings about being forsaken by God. The unpardonable sin must be one of Satan's favorite instruments for torturing the saints, because there are so many people with the same scars on their souls. How we need to learn this simple principle of discernment: the Holy Spirit of God is the Comforter, not the Tormentor.

Should some reader right now be in the anguishing throes of uncertainty (or even entertaining lingering doubts) concerning his salvation, may I assure you God's grace is greater than any sin you may have committed or any failure you may have made. The very fact that you are concerned about your relationship with God is an indication the Holy Spirit is faithfully drawing you into the love and forgiveness of Jesus. I say this with assurance—for I speak not only from my own experience, but that of countless counseling sessions with individuals who felt precisely as you do right now.

When Jesus cried out upon the cross, "It is finished," that included Satan's power to accuse and condemn the children of God! Your relationship with God as your Savior is not based on how you feel, but upon His faithfulness. Don't be among those who are going to worry themselves all the way to heaven. Make God's sure word your continuing confession:

> There is therefore no condemnation to those who are in Christ Jesus. . . . He that hears my (Christ's) word and believes on Him who sent Me has *everlasting* life, and shall *not* come into condemnation; but is passed from death into life. . . . For God has not given us a spirit of fear; but of power, and of love and of a sound mind. (Rom. 8:1; John 5:24; II Tim. 1:7 various versions)

Satan knows if he can paralyze our faith by overwhelming feelings of fear or guilt, he has effectively weakened our walk in the Spirit, and completely neutralized our witness concerning God's love and grace. Let us therefore allow our inner man to be totally flooded by God's Spirit of light and love, for darkness and fear are thereby dispelled and held at abeyance. May we throw off the yoke of condemnation and confess the Lordship of our Christ!

> There is no fear in love; but perfect love casteth out fear: because fear hath torment. . . . Beloved, if our heart condemn us not then we have confidence toward God. And whatsoever we ask, we receive of him. (I John 4:18; 3:21–22)

Feelings of fear and condemnation may recur, but if we claim the power of God's Spirit and the Lordship of His Son, we need not give way to such feelings. I recall counseling and praying with one individual several times before he finally accepted and confessed his complete victory in Christ. He was a rather brilliant person and persisted in reasoning his way back into condemnation. We quench the reassuring witness within of God's Spirit if we confess the lies of the Accuser rather than the promises of our High Priest, who "ever liveth to make intercession" on our behalf (Heb. 7:25).

Curiosity

Curiosity is the function of the soul which relates to our natural desires to inquire and explore the unknown. It reaches its most sophisticated levels perhaps in the pursuit of science. The scientific method is designed to enable men to effectively investigate the unknowns of our natural world and universe beyond.

The spirit of inquiry may be noble or perverted depending upon the attitude and purpose of the investigator and the object of his curiosity. The angels long to look into the mystery of salvation; the disciples were curious about the Kingdom of God and asked Jesus many questions. On the other hand, many instances of curiosity, especially in the Old Testament, referred to divinely forbidden areas. I suppose it all began with Eve's curiosity concerning the tree of knowledge. It has extended into all of the various practices of the occult. Satan's substitute for those who react to a materialistic philosophy is a sweep in the opposite direction to spiritualism and the mysterious realm of the occult. The Scriptures have many references to witchcraft, divination, sorcery, necromancy, magic, and even astrology. In each case, God's intense disapproval is directed toward such abominations (Exod. 22:18; Lev. 19:26, 31; 20:6, 27; Deut. 4:19; 13:1–5; II Kings 9:22; 21:2–6; 23:24; I Chron. 10:13–14; Isa. 8:19; 47:9, 12–14; Jer. 8:1–2; 14:14; 19:13; 27:9–10; 29:8–9; Zeph. 1:4–6; Acts 16:16–18; 19:19; Gal. 3:1–3; 4:10–11; 5:19–21; Rev. 9:20–21; 18:23; 21:8; 22:14–15).

A few Spirit-filled Christians, recognizing the reality of the spirit realm, have been deceived into investigating psychic phenomena with the thought of controlling such powers for divine purpose. Their thesis is that extrasensory perception (ESP) and related phenomena are natural endowments which can be used for either evil or good; therefore, they require investigation by open-minded individuals. Deceived themselves, such leaders can convincingly and sincerely deceive others, all within a very beguiling pseudo-charismatic context. They emphasize the need for honest inquiry into the psychic realm with an attitude free from prejudice. An atmosphere of love and tolerance mixed with much truth provides the background for these false prophets to effectively operate as angels of light, but the company they keep and the practices they follow noticeably grade off into outright spiritism.

Witchcraft (sorcery) is listed as one of the works of the flesh (Gal. 5:20). This refers to the *soulish* fascination one finds in personally pursuing the intriguing mysteries of the spirit and psychic world. Not everything in the supernatural realm is of God. Satan has counterfeits for all of the gifts of the Spirit, but ultimately they lead to spiritual darkness rather than blessing.

There is a clean simplicity and purity of Spirit in genuine movings of God. The simplicity and purity are related to becoming better acquainted with Jesus in a wholesome way. There is a divine mystery to the incarnation, but the biblical record of Christ's life does not have a spooky-spiritual quality to it.

The apostle Paul expresses a concern in his second letter to the Corinthian church:

> I am frightened, fearing that in some way you will be led away from your pure and simple devotion to our Lord, just as Eve was deceived by Satan in the Garden of Eden. You seem so gullible: you believe whatever anyone tells you even if he is preaching about another Jesus than the one we preach, or a different spirit than the Holy Spirit you received, or shows you a different way to

be saved. You swallow it all. . . . God never sent these men to you at all; they are "phonies" who have fooled you into thinking they are Christ's apostles. Yet I am not surprised! Satan can change himself into an angel of light, so it is no wonder his servants can do it too, and seem like godly ministers. (II Cor. 11:3-4, 13-15 TLB).

Perception

Perception is that function of the soul whereby information from the sense world is registered at the level of consciousness and interpreted in terms of its significance. This obviously would involve the overlapping functions of other soulish faculties (reason, memory, curiosity, etc.). The powers of *reception* may be perfect (twenty-twenty vision) but the powers of *perception* may be poor (absentmindedly running a redlight).

For some, perception is developed only to the extent that will bring them physical pleasure or spare them physical pain. More refined individuals would pursue the realm of aesthetics —the beauty of literature, music, art, nature, etc.—but still within the limited framework of selfish, soulish satisfaction. Those with a keen sense of social justice will be most perceptive to the needs and wants of others. This, too, can be at a soulish level, unrelated to their spiritual need and concern.

The problems of society stem basically from an inner spiritual sickness and poverty. Yet social and spiritual needs are so closely interrelated, one can't truly be separated from the other. The Enemy would seek to blind us to both if possible; short of this, he would have us focus on one without the other, knowing the limitation such a divorce will bring to both. Meeting the natural needs of men *in the name of Jesus* can build the bridge across which the good news of eternal life can most sympathetically come.

Another aspect of perception deals with its relationship to faith. Faith lifts us beyond the limitations of the sense world of circumstances. We are enabled to relate the earthly and temporal to the heavenly and eternal. Faith releases and directs the perfecting power of God's Spirit in our daily lives—in other words, faith works where we live.

The apostle Paul has provided a precise definition:

> Faith is the substance (confident assurance—solid ground) of things hoped for, the evidence (conviction and perception) of things not seen. (Heb. 11:1 various versions)

The eye of faith (spiritual vision) *perceives* as here and now that which is not yet evident to the natural eye. Faith breaks the time and place barrier and gives us peace in our present natural situation.

The Deceiver desires to shift our faith from the *spiritual* realm to the *sensual* realm and tempts us to measure everything in terms of our apparent circumstances. The Holy Spirit of Truth desires to wash out our spiritual eyes and ears that we might see and hear our Good Shepherd when our natural valleys are both dark and deathly silent.

Even as I write, God is applying this truth to some areas of keen concern in my own life. I stopped writing and specifically thanked the Lord for renewing my faith and settling my soul in the certainty of His Word and the faithfulness of His Spirit. Some of you may want to do the same thing right now.

Jesus never gauged things as they seemed in the natural. He looked beneath the surface of men's lives to their inner need; He listened beyond their spoken words to the cry of their hearts; He reached below the hard shell of their outer defenses to the hurt within—this is true spiritual perception. Rather obviously, our natural and spiritual senses are to be closely linked when it comes to our walk of faith. Only the welding power of God's Spirit can accomplish such a union, and this is what Spirit Baptism is all about. This, again, is what it means for the inner man to get wet all over.

Memory

The memory is the function of the soul which enables us to recall the past. There is probably a continual flow from the reservoir of memory which mixes with our streams of current thought and feeling. Our responses to existing situations are conditioned by past experience. In fact, what we are today is an accumulation of everything that has happened in all of our yesterdays. We are a product of the past. The significance of this in regard to Holy Spirit Baptism will be the topic of our next chapter.

The memory is a vast storehouse of information and experience from the past. It is like a large iceberg in that only a small portion of our thought life is above the level of consciousness. Most of our mind is below the water in the realm of the subconscious. We can plug in to the main current of thought by connecting appropriate circuits from our memory bank. For instance, we can very quickly and accurately bring to our attention a needed portion of the multiplication table—or our address and phone number.

Some information from the past is buried so deeply it is difficult to recall. Other items were never secured very firmly in the first place, and have long-since faded away. The more a memory circuit is used, the easier it is to bring it into the realm of conscious thought. Some things can be purposely suppressed to inhibit their influence upon our thought-life. We are what we think (Prov. 23:7), and obviously some control is essential. Soulish suppression, however, can create more problems than it solves.

The Scriptures repeatedly encourage us to remember some things, and forget others:

Remember his marvellous works that he hath done, his wonders, and the judgments of his mouth. (I Chron. 16:12)

Remember ye not the former things, neither consider the things of old. Behold, I will do a new thing; now it shall spring forth; shall ye not know it? (Isa. 43:18–19)

The Psalms, particularly, have many exhortations concerning the role of memory in the life of God's saints. Many of our problems arise from forgetting and remembering the wrong things. A study of the words "forget" and "remember" and their derivation in Scripture is most revealing and personally profitable. To put into practice what we learn concerning thought control is something else again. Very quickly we will realize our need of a power beyond our own if we are going to effectively harness our minds for God's glory. Some of us need a spiritual shock treatment and a complete rewiring job!

SUPREMACY: SPIRIT VERSUS SOUL

It is apparent that there is to be a continual interaction between the energized spirit of man and his soul, wherein the soul becomes subject through the human spirit to the direction and power of God's Spirit. Satan's desire is to divorce the soul from the supremacy of the spirit. The specific functions of man's spirit are then reduced to soulish (and lifeless) activities. A review of the spiritual functions will make this clear:

A. Revelation
  1. Soulish supremacy
     Under the reign of the soul, revelation shifts into the realm of mystical fantasy and speculation. Spiritual pride disconnects such soulish endeavor from the correcting counsel which the Body of Christ can provide. Satan is then supplied with the opportunity to fire the imagination with spurious dreams, visions, divisive doctrines, and distracting signs.
  2. Spiritual supremacy
     Truth floods into our lives as the life-producing light of God's love. With it comes a sense of direction and a desire to obey

and fulfill the will of the Lord *with* our brothers and sisters in Christ. The result is a wholesome unity within and an effective witness without.

B. Prayer and worship
   1. Soulish supremacy
      Prayer is reduced to a lifeless—though perhaps loud, long, and flowery—form. It can also so emphasize the negative side of need that more darkness is produced than light. I have felt worse after some prayers than I did before. (Mine as well as those of others.)
      Worship loses its spontaneity and becomes a spiritless ritual. The lack of spiritual life, however, can cleverly be disguised by our being deceived into thinking soulish stimulation is divine inspiration. Noble or entertaining ideas may stir our minds, and rhythmic music may move our hearts, but this is no indication that our souls have necessarily been inspired. Only the Holy Spirit can inspire us to true worship; all else is soulish activity.
   2. Spiritual supremacy
      When the Spirit rules supreme, prayer becomes as alive as the one to whom we pray. With sensitivity to God's will and confidence in His faithfulness, our prayers will be both positive and specific. Praise purifies our soul and releases the power of God's presence in our lives. Worship is filled with understanding and affection, and we are refreshed by the Comforter Himself.

C. Communion
   1. Soulish supremacy.
      Communion with God that once led us to praise and worship becomes communion with nature, the fine arts, or even the mystical, in a way which leads only to self-satisfaction. Solitude involves isolation from the Lord as well as society, and we are left with only the musings of our own minds.
   2. Spiritual supremacy
      The Holy Spirit provides the atmosphere whereby there can be intimate times of sweet fellowship with the Lord. Inner peace and healing of a spiritual nature bring soundness to our souls. There can be a silent solitude of spirit even in the midst of the noisy multitude. There are times when we say nothing

and He says nothing. Nothing needs to be said, for all is well with our soul.

D. Witness (Ministry)
　1. Soulish supremacy
　　Witness to men apart from the Holy Spirit becomes as loveless as it is lifeless. Truth can be coldly sterile without the heartbeat of God to go with it. I remember someone saying once they had really "nailed" a young man to the wall with their knowledge of Scripture. It is possible to kill people with the very truth that was given in love for life.
　2. Spiritual supremacy
　　Our witness to others develops from a natural (yet supernatural) desire to simply share the life of Jesus with those about us who need to know His love for them. Our witness is based on a sincere interest in them as persons whom God loves. It may begin as a cup of cold water, or a refreshing smile, but all in the name of Jesus. Love, truth, and faith are the ingredients which the Holy Spirit needs for an effective witness He can bless.

E. Discernment
　1. Soulish supremacy
　　Discernment either develops into a suspicious, critical spirit or becomes deadened to the point of uselessness. Either extreme is dangerous. Truth without love can even lead to a subtle judgmental attitude which is forever trying to discern how soulish or spiritual everybody else is.
　2. Spiritual supremacy
　　The predominant purpose for true spiritual discernment is to recognize the will and way of God. What is apart from this can then be readily detected along with the redemptive measures the Lord would desire to use to re-center an off-center situation. Both the fruit and gifts of the Spirit are essential in bringing healing to unwholesome situations: humility, love, long-suffering, self-control, faith, obedience, prayer, and decisive action. The result is the clean, pure, will and work of God.

F. Fellowship
　1. Soulish supremacy
　　The Fellowship can drift from sharing around the Lord to a

purely social function where Christ is pushed further and further to the periphery of our interest. Togetherness becomes an end in itself devoid of divine purpose.

2. Spiritual supremacy

Spiritual fellowship requires a unifying *purpose* and a unifying *power*. The purpose is the glorious life of Jesus Christ, and the power is the harmonizing ministry of the Holy Spirit. He joyfully yokes us to Christ and one another in a maturing, life-releasing family fellowship which the Father has lovingly planned to last forever. As we find our place and function in the Body of Christ, the Holy Spirit can release our full potential as the beautiful persons we were created to be.

G. Warfare

1. Soulish supremacy

Warfare with Satan is reduced to personal attacks upon people because they are easier to see when our spiritual vision is dim. We will tend to react in a soulish way to situations of conflict rather than respond in the Spirit with a redemptive purpose in view. The result is tragic for all concerned—except Satan.

2. Spiritual supremacy

We can confront spiritual conflict with confidence when we realize the defensive and offensive equipment which is ours. To know the Enemy and his strategies and the counter-strategies of God's Spirit gives us a divine boldness to engage and overcome the devil on any front where he may choose to attack. Furthermore, we can aggressively take the initiative and challenge the Enemy on the very ground which he falsely claims is his own.

Conclusion

How very encouraging it is to realize that the Baptism of Jesus in the Holy Spirit is to saturate the inner man (spirit-soul) with the transforming power of God's truth and love. The baptismal waters are ever flowing, for God's Spirit is ever moving. Through faith and obedience, we can move with the stream, and it can move through us—all the time, everywhere, in everything, and with everyone. Indeed, every inch of our life is to experience the releasing power of the Holy Spirit. This is to include the past as well as the present—this will be the theme of our next chapter.

6

HOLY SPIRIT BAPTISM: PART THREE

A Healing Stream

Fling off the dirty clothes of the old way of living, which were rotted through and through with lust's illusions, and, with yourselves mentally and spiritually remade . . . put on the clean fresh clothes of the new life which was made by God's design for righteousness and the holiness which is no illusion. (Eph. 4:22–24 Phillips)

May He grant you out of the rich treasury of His glory to be strengthened and reinforced with mighty power in the inner man by the Holy Spirit Himself—indwelling your innermost being and personality. May Christ through your faith actually dwell in your hearts; that your roots may go down deep into the soil of God's marvelous love.

And I pray that you will come to know through personal experience the breadth, length, depth and height of Christ's unfathomable love; that you may be filled and flooded through all your being with the fulness of God Himself. (Eph. 3:16–19 various versions)

FLOODED WITH GOD'S LIGHT AND LOVE

The Baptism of Jesus in the Holy Spirit is to flood our inner man (spirit and soul) to overflowing with the healing power of

God's love. It would be good to picture yourselves as standing at the feet of Jesus and allowing Him who is the light of the world to bathe our lives with the light of God's love and truth. I have sometimes thought of myself as being perfectly transparent in the light of His presence—allowing no area of my life to be unexposed to the clean, pure, bright, revealing and releasing light of the Lord.

Only light can dispel darkness! Fighting, arguing, pleading, or bluffing will not push darkness out of our lives. Nor is there an escape by running or hiding, for the darkness is within, not without. Only light—an inner light—can dispel the shadows of the spirit and soul. But when it comes, the darkness goes, and all the things that live in the darkness go with it. If you have ever turned over a rock or a board in the bright noonday sun, you may have noticed all kinds of little creatures scurrying about, trying to escape the light—for they are residents of the darkness. So it is when the light of God's love and truth shines into every corner, crevice, nook, and cranny of our world within. Both the darkness and the powers of darkness must flee before the light of God's Holy and Almighty Spirit.

Once when praying for a woman that her life might be flooded with the brilliant light of God's Spirit, I felt I could see windows lighting up all throughout a darkened house. I realized it meant God was moving about through every room in the home of her heart. His very presence dispelled the darkness, and her spirit and soul became aglow with the love, joy, and peace of the Lord:

> Once your heart was full of darkness, but now it is full of light from the Lord. Therefore live and act as sons of the light. (Eph. 5:8 various versions)

> Ye are all the children of light, and the children of the day: we are not of the night, nor of darkness. (I Thess. 5:5)

Take heed, as unto a light that shineth in a dark place, until the day dawn, and the day star arise in your hearts. (II Pet. 1:19)

Then shall your light break forth as the morning, and your healing [your restoration and the power of a new life] shall spring forth speedily; your righteousness . . . shall go before you [conducting you to peace and prosperity], and the glory of the Lord shall be your rear guard. (Isa. 58:8 TAB)

Returning from a weekend retreat, a woman in the back seat of our host's automobile mentioned her fear of a recurring depression of mind. She had recently passed through the darkness of a nervous breakdown, and was afraid this cloud of apprehension was the herald for another inner storm. The Lord provided a prophetic word for her encouragement:

My daughter you are not to fear; for the clouds you see are not the indication of an impending storm with its darkness and violence, but only the mists of the morning—the leftovers from the night—which shall soon fade away, for the Sun of Righteousness arises for you with healing in His wings!

She was in a time of spiritual, mental, and physical recovery, and the Lord wanted to reassure a lovely handmaiden of God of His protecting and healing presence. The Enemy was trying to torment her with memories from the past.

The Memorial Library of Our Mind

We are a product of the past. What we are today is an accumulation of all our yesterdays—each of which has been carefully filed in the storehouse of our memory. Therefore, a baptism of the inner man will need to include the past as well as the present. This poses no problem for the Eternal Spirit of God, for our blessed Comforter can readily break the time-barrier at will. The streams of the Spirit are capable of surging and searching back into the most remote reaches of our memories and into the deepest recesses of our subconscious mind.

It was mentioned in our last chapter that the unconscious part of our mind is like the hidden portion of a great iceberg which lies below the surface of the waters. Information is continually being stored in and retrieved from this vast library of our subconscious. Some of the volumes are used daily, others less frequently. Some date back to early childhood, and the print has long since faded from the pages, except for those portions of the script where the impression was deep and dark.

Many of our memory books have bright, cheerful covers, and their happy contents have been read and re-read with much joy and profit. Others are more somber in appearance, and a glance at some of the well-worn, but tearstained pages, reminds us that there have been past sorrows as well as joys. Some of these darker and heavier volumes have a way of crossing the counterline of our consciousness without being called for, and the pages have a persistent way of falling open to the same places over and over again. The print is large and black and can be read at a glance. Each page is profusely illustrated with vivid pictures which are most painful and depressing. One never knows when such a volume is going to turn up.

There is also a room in which memory books of a forbidden nature are kept securely locked away. This area is never available to our consciousness unless under extreme pressure the locks are broken. Although the room is located in the basement of our memorial library, it is a very active and productive place. It is true, specific volumes are not allowed to come to the counterline of consciousness, but they do provide resource material for the publication of bulletins which get mixed in with all the other books in the entire library. The content of the bulletins is carefully disguised so their sources cannot be detected. The mental, emotional, and physical response to the material, however, is as devastating as that which would be produced by the forbidden memory volume itself.

One might hope for a more authoritative control over the storage-retrieval process. Further remedial action could involve the elimination of all the detrimental volumes and their replacement by some new works of a different author. Even the reference works in the forbidden area might be rewritten in such a way as to relieve the content of its tormenting, pain-inducing qualities and allow the remaining information to have a truly redemptive purpose. What a glorious renovation of our memorial library this would be!

The Time-line of Life

The allegory in the above section is obvious: the subconscious mind of man needs the renovating power which only the Holy Spirit Himself can administer to our lives. The thorough way in which the Comforter desires to reach the various phases of our past is illustrated in the diagram on the following page.

The time-line of our lives can be divided into a series of distinctive phases which we usually break into rather abruptly. The entrance into each new segment of life involves appropriate adjustments—spiritual, psychological, and sometimes even physical. Transition points are times of opportunity and danger. We become exposed to a whole new set of circumstances involving different people, places, things, privileges, responsibilities, desires, and decisions. An element of uncertainty is always associated with the unknown. Confidence develops as we learn not only to cope with, but in a measure control a new situation. We must learn not only how to steer ourselves through a new and different world, but to exert a directing influence on that world as well. It is like learning to build a road and drive on it, too.

Occasionally the shock of entry into a new phase of life

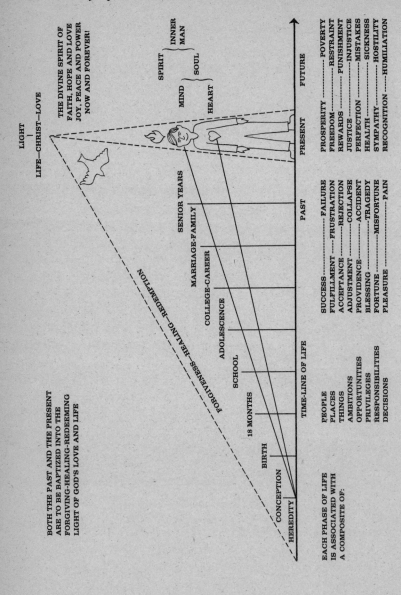

leaves a lasting scar which is persistently painful. The memory of that experience can undermine our faith and confidence for any new venture which God would have for us—whether it be in the realm of schooling, employment, marriage, or some specific mission for the Lord. Sometimes the hurdle of entrance is successfully crossed, but unexpected tragedy strikes and cuts short or drastically alters our progress in that area of our lives. The consequences can color (or discolor) all other phases of our lives which are to follow.

Weed Patch or Fruitful Garden

The present is the seedbed into which the events of our daily lives are sown. There are the seeds of success and seeds of failure; of achievement and frustration; appreciation and depreciation; acceptance and rejection; acclaim and humiliation; victory and defeat; fortune and misfortune; harmony and hostility; health and sickness; life and death—and many more! Each seed sends roots deep into our hearts and minds from which a plant develops and eventually bears fruit. The fruit may be bitter or sweet, depending upon the character of the seed.

Well-rooted, long-established weeds are not easily removed. One may cut the tops off and obtain temporary results, but new growth stubbornly reappears—a lesson I once learned when our grass became infested with dandelions. Everything looked fine after mowing, but in a few days the whole lawn was in full bloom again. I discovered the best solution was to root out the large taproot characteristic of dandelions and replace the hole with a sprig of grass. The application is obvious; we may be blessed in an inspirational meeting somewhere and feel fine for a few days, only to find that the same old life problems reappear again to plague our every step. Evidently something needs to be thoroughly rooted out and replaced with the fruit-producing seed of God's Spirit if we want lasting results. This is the purpose of divine deliverance.

Our Threefold Salvation

Salvation in Christ Jesus has an eternal quality to it which can reach into the past, present, and future. There is also a threefold ministry of the Holy Spirit which is to apply God's saving and delivering power to our lives. The Lord wants not only to *forgive* our past, but *heal* it as well! Furthermore, the past is also to be *redeemed* for God's glorious purpose in our lives for the future. Past mistakes, failures, and even tragedies are a part of the "all things" which God promised He would work together for our good if we continue to *love* Him and are committed to His ongoing purpose for our lives (Rom 8:28).

The forgiving-healing-redeeming power of God's Holy Spirit is illustrated by an experience which was shared with me during a recent trip abroad. A young girl in her twenties, whom we shall call Penny, was introduced to me during a time of deep depression in her life. Penny had recently been converted to the Lord and baptized by Jesus in the Holy Spirit. However, she was haunted by a tragedy which had occurred while she was a member of the Hell's Angels. She had accidentally killed a child while riding her motorcycle, and while she knew in her head she was *forgiven*, the hurt in her heart still needed to be *healed*.

Through tears of anguish she told me how she had begged and pleaded with God to protect her from future situations which would in any way remind her of this tragic incident. Yet on their way up to the retreat, they had stopped to pick up a hitchhiker. In the course of their witness to him concerning the love of God in Christ Jesus, he shared something of his past life with them. It so closely paralleled Penny's experience, that all the old wounds of her past life had been painfully reopened. This was the immediate cause for her intense distress.

Here was a handmaiden of God who was haunted by a memory which needed to be healed by Jesus through the power of His indwelling Spirit—and this was the basis on which we shared with her. I assured her God was going to give her the desire of her heart—to be spared the pain from her past—but in a way going far beyond her expectation. Her Great Physician was going to not only *heal* her wounded heart, but *redeem* that portion of her life so it actually could become a means of effective witness. God doesn't just wrest the weapon of torment from the Enemy's hand; but He replaces it in our hand that it might become a powerful instrument for our victory and His glory.

As we laid hands upon Penny and confessed the releasing, redeeming power of God's Holy Spirit, a mighty inner baptism was completed in her life, and darkness and depression were replaced with the healing oil of gladness. She laughed and cried and worshiped the Lord in her heavenly tongue of praise. It was a joyful occasion all the way around—everybody got wet in the overflow.

The Lord graciously confirmed the reality of her experience a day or so later when a group of the young people went to a nearby village to share their faith. While there they ran into a group of Hell's Angels, and Penny discovered the redeeming power of God's grace is all-sufficient. She not only did not panic, but laughingly stuck "Jesus stickers" all over the bike riders' leather jackets and invited them to the meetings. (Several came the last evening and were quite overwhelmed by the love of God's people.)

Something else happened the last night of the retreat that proved that God can both *heal* and *redeem* the most tragic scars from the past. A couple came to the evening meeting partly intoxicated. Several took them aside and began to share with them concerning God's love. Penny felt strangely drawn to join the group. She arrived just as the man was saying with much sorrow of heart, "But you don't understand—I have gone too far. You see, I have killed someone, and none of you would even know what I have gone through!" To his surprise, he heard the strong, convincing voice of a young woman reply, "But I do understand, for I have been down that road myself, and that is where I met Jesus. You can meet Him too!" Yes, God not only forgives, but He also heals. Furthermore, He not only heals; but He also redeems. And what His Spirit has done for others, He can do for you—even as you read this chapter.

Walking With Jesus Down Memory's Lane

There is no part of our past life that we need fear if we walk along memory's lane hand-in-hand with the Lord Jesus Himself. It is the purpose of our Blessed Comforter to make the Lord very real to us as our Great Physician. He knows us better than we know ourselves and can perfectly diagnose our inner sickness of soul and spirit and is Himself the healing we need. He is not distracted by symptoms, but powerfully and precisely searches out the very source of our infected past and removes the entire cancer, roots and all. He then counsels and prepares us for our time of convalescence and recovery. The area may remain tender for a time, but the disease is gone—the infection is out—and we have the privilege and responsibility of cooperating with the recovery routine which assures us of renewed health and strength within. He, indeed, "restoreth our souls."

Before considering some of the problems related to different life phases, let us further establish the principle of the healing Christ. How can we get Jesus back into the past parts of our lives where His healing presence is needed most? One approach is through the doorway of a sanctified imagination.

For so long Satan has had free access to our souls by way of our imagination, why can't we invite Jesus to come through the same door? Actually, this is an expression of faith which releases the power of God's Spirit in a way that far exceeds what might be accomplished by just the power of our positive thinking!

We can trust the Holy Spirit to imprint within our minds the "image" of Jesus standing by our side with an expression of loving care and concern in His eyes. There is a sense of command and authority about His presence which is not austere, but warmly reassuring. He takes us by the hand and beckons us to walk with Him side-by-side as together we proceed into the obvious highways and the more obscure byways of our past life. There is a sense of safety and inner peace which His presence and loving touch always brings. (This actually is almost a word-for-word description of a vision which was related to me by a sister in Christ who had recently passed through a shadowed valley.)

There are no memory lanes which we need fear to take with the Lord by our side. Even well-worn trails of tears can be transformed into paths of peace by His redeeming Presence. We may even open gates which we have consciously or subconsciously locked and posted with "No Trespassing" signs. In fact, the Lord will encourage us to enter with Him some of the "haunted houses" of regret which we have carefully avoided over the intervening months and years. With Him we can draw the drapes, open wide the windows, and allow the fresh breath of God's Spirit and the light of God's love to dispel the dark, musty atmosphere which has been so stifling for so long. What has been a curse to our soul, can become a blessing and a place of profit—when visited by the Lord.

Specifically, this means we can face fearful, painful experiences in our past which we have purposely tried to seal off from our thinking. The Holy Spirit can remove the hurt and sorrow from these memories and actually redeem that part of our past for His glorious present-time purpose through our lives. This is more than wishful or sentimental thinking, for God has promised to turn our mourning into dancing, put off our sackcloth, and gird us with gladness and also to give us "beauty for ashes, the oil of joy for mourning, the garment of praise for the spirit of heaviness; that [we] might be called trees of righteousness, the planting of the Lord, that he might be glorified" (Ps. 30:11; Isa. 61:3).

The *healing-redeeming* work of Christ is the same yesterday as it is today, and will be forever (Heb. 13:8). This truth is illustrated by a testimony of deliverance which I heard while attending a seminar on spiritual healing. A young woman had been plagued for years by nightmares. During a time of spiritual counseling, she was willing to identify the source of her problem. (Sometimes only the Holy Spirit can help us recognize our underlying needs.) At the age of four or five, she had undergone a serious emotional shock. A tramp had gained entrance to her home, and when it became apparent he was about to be discovered, he found his way into her bedroom and hid under her bed. Her parents finally discovered him, and after an unpleasant conversation, he was forced to leave the house—but he left a little girl whose soul was scarred by fear.

For years the memory of this episode had been a source of torment to the young woman who still had something of a frightened little girl locked within her breast. The incident was persistently pressed back into her subconscious, for the memory was still *alive* with intense emotion. Her dreams were a heart-cry for relief and comfort. How could Jesus reach the little girl *within* with His healing love?

Her counselor was divinely guided to suggest that she walk back into the past with Jesus by her side and actually re-live the experience. She was encouraged in her mind to imagine how different the story might have been if the Lord had really been there. It was suggested that she look under the bed with Jesus and relate the results of that confrontation now that He was included in the scene.

After a short time of silence, the counselor inquired if she and Jesus had looked under the bed together. "No," she replied, "I knew who was there, so I asked Jesus to look for Himself." "Then what happened?" asked the counselor. The young woman responded in a very triumphant way, "Why, we called in my parents and told them to get out our best silver and dishes and set the table for dinner, for a very special guest had come to visit." Needless to say, there were no more nightmares.

PRINCIPLE: OVERCOME EVIL WITH GOOD

Some years ago, soon after I became aware of God's desire to release His children who have been imprisoned by the past, I faced my first opportunity to pray for a healing of memories. A lady approached me with her face darkened by fear and anxiety and asked me to pray for her deliverance. I explained how the God of Eternity could reach into her past, and by the releasing power of His love and truth, set her spirit free.

The Lord prompted me to employ the principle of overcoming evil with good. The streams of God's Holy Spirit were presented as sweeping through her past life and touching with Christ's healing power every person, place, thing, and/or event which in any way contributed to her present state of anxiety. Where there was darkness, delusion, and depression, Christ was bringing His light, truth, and deliverance. Fear, doubt, and distress were giving way to the holy streams of faith, hope, and love. Pride, jealousy, resentment, and self-pity were being rooted out by God's releasing power and replanted with the fruit of humility, forgiveness, and compassion. As we prayed together, we pictured her life being flooded with the peace and joy of Christ's ever-flowing Spirit of life.

God's power and glory suddenly rested upon her, and she actually fell from her chair to the floor and burst out praising God in a heavenly tongue of joyful worship. Her first praises in English some time later were most moving: "Oh, my Redeemer, my Lord, and my King . . . Welcome home, Oh, welcome home!" Her husband later said it was the first time he had seen her smile in many weeks. It was a beautiful introduction for us both to the Spirit's ministry of inner healing.

The overcoming-evil-with-good principle is a positive spiritual truth concerning the displacing power of God's Holy Spirit. Just as only light can displace darkness, only love can displace hate. To try to push out evil without the displacing work of the Spirit only leads to frustration and disappointment. The beauty of Holy Spirit Baptism for the believer is seen in a more lovely light than ever before. Here is the power that enables us to bear witness concerning the liberated life which we possess in Christ Jesus.

The displacing power of the Holy Spirit is best appreciated by specifically contrasting the forces for both evil and good. The couplet series to follow specifically defines some of the dark shadows of the soul which are effectively dispelled by the light of God's Holy Spirit. The first member in each pair is overcome by the second. I must admit in preparing the following list I discovered the Lord was re-searching my soul afresh with the purpose of further healing in view. The list is not just to be read over, but faithfully prayed through. A suggested form follows:

"Heavenly Father, in the name of Jesus Christ I confess that Your Spirit of light is this very moment dispelling the shadow of darkness in my life. I praise and thank You!"

As one proceeds through the list with this attitude of heart,

God's Spirit will highlight the particular areas of healing that He desires for our lives. Following the completion of the next chapter, you might wish to return to the list with added understanding of how the Holy Spirit will relate the shadows to particular places, people, and incidents of the past, all within the healing light of Christ's Holy Spirit.

"A" is *overcome* and *displaced* by "B":

A	B
1. Darkness	Light
2. Delusion	Reality
3. Error	Truth
4. Deception	Discernment
5. Deceit	Honesty
6. Pride	Humility
7. Arrogance	Meekness
8. Insolence	Respect
9. Rebellion	Submission
10. Defiance	Compliance
11. Stubbornness	Adaptability
12. Hostility	Reconciliation
13. Antagonism	Compatability
14. Enmity	Friendliness
15. Prejudice	Fairness
16. Bigotry	Tolerance
17. Rudeness	Courtesy
18. Harshness	Gentleness
19. Pushiness	Forbearance
20. Argumentation	Agreement
21. Contention	Cooperation
22. Strife	Unity
23. Discord	Harmony
24. Conflict	Pacification
25. Contempt	Honor
26. Complaint	Commendation
27. Division	Communion
28. Hostility	Reconciliation
29. Turmoil	Peace
30. Agitation	Rest

31. Impatience	Long-suffering
32. Judgment	Understanding
33. Criticism	Praise
34. Suspicion	Trust
35. Jealousy	Admiration
36. Envy	Contentment
37. Greed	Benevolence
38. Stinginess	Generosity
39. Selfishness	Sharing
40. Resentment	Forgiveness
41. Revenge	Blessing
42. Retaliation	Apology
43. Anger	Temperance
44. Hatred	Love
45. Cruelty	Kindness
46. Grief	Comfort
47. Sorrow	Consolation
48. Sadness	Joy
49. Moodiness	Stability
50. Melancholy	Cheerfulness
51. Grumbling	Thanksgiving
52. Self-pity	Compassion
53. Doubt	Faith
54. Fear	Courage
55. Depression	Elation
56. Discouragement	Incentive
57. Despair	Hope
58. Defeat	Victory
59. Failure	Success
60. Pessimism	Optimism
61. Frustration	Fulfillment
62. Bondage	Freedom
63. Limitation	Release
64. Slavery	Liberty
65. Cowardice	Boldness
66. Self-depreciation	Godly esteem
67. Inferiority	Equality
68. Guilt	Grace
69. Isolation	Fellowship
70. Procrastination	Punctuality

71. Indecision	Commitment
72. Indifference	Responsibility
73. Irresponsibility	Reliability
74. Carelessness	Concern
75. Laziness	Zeal
76. Hardheadedness	Teachableness

The two lists could also be headed: "Weeds of the Devil" and "Fruit of the Spirit." The Holy Spirit has provided us with all of the tools (Gifts of the Spirit) and the seed (Fruit of the Spirit) which are needed for a fragrant and fruitful garden for God's purpose and pleasure. It will require both hoeing and planting, but every provision for abundant life in the garden of our hearts was purchased for us on Calvary. God wants very much for us to experience a life of liberty as He planned it for us in Christ Jesus. It is *His* will and *our* privilege.

7

HOLY SPIRIT BAPTISM: PART FOUR

Power in Practice

And we have come to understand and to trust the love that God has for us. God is love . . . (and) we love Him because He first loved us. There is no fear in love; but perfect love *expels* fear, because fear has torment. (I John 4:16, 19, 18 various versions)

For God has not given us a spirit of fear, but of *power* and of *love* and of a *sound mind*. (II Tim. 1:7 various versions)

God will guard and keep him in perfect and constant peace whose *mind* is stayed on Him, because he commits himself to God. So trust in the Lord—commit yourself to Him—forever; for the Lord God is an everlasting rock—the Rock of ages. (Isa. 26:3-4 TAB, modified)

Do not worry about anything, but *tell* God every detail of your needs in earnest and thankful prayer. And the peace of God which surpasses all comprehension will guard and keep your *hearts* and *minds* in Christ Jesus. (Phil. 4:6-7 various versions)

And it shall come to pass, that before they call, I *will* answer; and while they are yet speaking, I *will* hear. (Isa. 65:24)

He sent his word, and *healed* them, and *delivered* them from their destructions. (Ps. 107:20)

ALL THINGS: PAST—PRESENT—FUTURE

What a relief it is to be able to face our past without fear. It is possible only as we are assured of God's everlasting love for His children—a love not based on our feelings, but on His faithfulness. Perfect love casts out fear; therefore it is with faith and hope that we can allow the Lord by His Spirit to fill every part of our past with His healing light. God has promised to perform every word He has spoken if we will submit to that word in faith and obedience. We can indeed see His power in practice.

It will be of interest to refer again to the various stages commonly associated with the time-line of life. As mentioned before, each phase possesses its own peculiar problems, often reinforced by the experiences of past phases. The roots of some painful and perplexing problems can be traced back to prior generations. We can inherit physical deficiencies and even certain mental/emotional disorders from our ancestors. Some traits are not directly inherited in a genetic way, but developed from the cultural or environmental atmosphere associated with our early family relationships. Actually, we are a product of our heredity and our culture (nature and nurture). The interactions can be very complex, but we can find real assurance in the knowledge that God understands us better than we do ourselves. Furthermore, He has promised that all things can be worked together for good.

We sometimes quote the familiar proverb, "Bad blood will tell!" but this does not take into account the redeeming-perfecting power which the blood of Christ can bring to our lives. We inherit a new nature in Jesus Christ, and through the ministry of the Holy Spirit, we can overcome any deficiency inherited from the past.

What the Lord does not *protect* us from concerning the past,

He will *deliver* us out of, or *perfect* us through. The good toward which God's Spirit works all things is the inner-image of Jesus Christ. There is nothing in the *past, present,* or *future* that the Holy Spirit cannot use to make us more like Jesus. Occasionally this involves an actually physical healing—sometimes it does not—but a spiritual (inner) healing is promised for all who will submit to the gracious ministry of God's Spirit. Physical healings are for time; spiritual healing is for eternity.

UNTO ALL GENERATIONS

During a family camp overseas, a young woman in her early twenties came to my attention. We shall call her Lydia. Lydia appeared to be painfully shy, and obviously withdrawn. I was informed that she was seriously depressed and desperately needed an inner spiritual healing. Most of the time she was alone, and even in the meetings, her downcast face showed little animation. She failed to share enthusiastically in any of the happy songs of worship, but sometimes—almost wistfully —her lips would softly follow the words. It hurt me to see the dull pain in her eyes while others about her sparkled for joy.

Toward the end of the week, one of the leaders and a personal friend encouraged Lydia to visit with us for a time of sharing and prayer. The opening moments were rather slow and unproductive, since she was too timid and withdrawn to spontaneously discuss her problem and supplied only one- or two-word answers to questions concerning her real needs. It seemed wise to establish a common ground of understanding, so I shared with her some painful experiences of my own past with which I felt she could readily identify. Our relationship became noticeably warmer, and she began to respond hesitantly to questions and sympathetic inquiries.

Lydia had met Christ as her Lord and Savior while she was in school. She was subsequently filled with the Holy Spirit.

Everything was satisfactory until she faced the demanding pressures of higher education. She was quite competent, but a number of stresses converged which evoked a state of severe depression.

Her warmest, closest family tie had been with her older sister who was married and had two children. A crisis developed during the birth of her second baby, and it was uncertain for a time if Lydia's sister would survive. Her mother had had a history of mental illness, and during this time of stress she broke down and was placed in an institution. Lydia was thirteen at the time, and it became her responsibility to care for her sister's first baby and maintain the household during much of the ordeal. Her sister recovered, but Lydia was left with a shadow in her life.

Under the stress of her current studies and examinations, pressure was again building up, and Lydia was haunted by an unconfessed fear. When the time was appropriate, I finally asked her if she was afraid that she had inherited her mother's mental and emotional weaknesses and was headed for a nervous breakdown. She admitted that this was her underlying fear. What a privilege it was to assure her that God's healing power could extend as far back into the inherited past as might be necessary to establish her security for the future—for His mercy endureth *unto all generations.*

We walked with her through the painful periods of her childhood and pictured the presence of Jesus in every situation. He would be to her an Elder Brother who would always be at her side to love, counsel, and support her. He would become her everlasting security, and she need never feel threatened again that someone she loved and looked up to would suddenly be taken away, leaving her with pressures of responsibility too great for her to handle. Her friend and I also assured her that there would always be brothers and sisters in the Lord who would be very near and ready to love and encourage her. Furthermore, in the future she would be able to help others who were facing situations similar to her own, for she could relate to them and they to her, and God's love could be shared with genuine compassion.

As we concluded in a healing prayer, confessing the Lordship of our Christ, the last shadows lifted, and a bright smile, which matched the sparkle in her eyes, assured us all that Jesus had done it again. The three of us joined our hearts and hands in praise and joyful worship. Lydia's happy conversation throughout the subsequent dinnertime was a beautiful contrast to the sorrowful silence of the preceding days.

Just before my departure two days later, Lydia joyfully approached me with the assurance that God had given her peace of heart and mind, and that she would be forever grateful to Him. The warm bright rays of the morning sun are most appreciated following an exceptionally dark and dismal night. It was a wonderful privilege to witness a sunrise in the life of one of God's lovely handmaidens.

Conceived in Love: Born with Blessing

The prenatal period between conception and birth may be more important than we realize in influencing our postnatal existence. There are many physical factors (nutrition, drugs, disease) which can adversely affect fetal development. When the drug scene first developed, some situations of acute postnatal distress were baffling until it was discovered that babies were suffering withdrawal symptoms after being separated from their drug-addicted mothers. Some people, while not addicted to alcohol or drugs, are intoxicated by fear, anger, or resentment. Such states of mind can definitely change our body chemistry in a detrimental way and actually produce psychosomatic (mind-body) diseases or aggravate other disorders. One wonders what effect such maternal distress might have upon the prenatal fetus. The Scriptures indicate the sins of those who hate God can influence their children unto the third and fourth generation (Exod 20:5).

There is a positive side, too, for God's mercy extends to a thousand generations for those who *love* and *obey* Him (Exod. 20:6). Prenatal love and prayer can be expected to provide a healthy spiritual and physical environment in which new life can reach for both its earthly and heavenly potential. I have always felt there was something significant along these lines in the account of Elizabeth's greeting upon the arrival of Mary (Luke 1:40–44). Mary saluted Elizabeth; Elizabeth's baby (John) leaped within her womb; Elizabeth was filled with the Spirit, and announced that her baby had leaped for joy upon the sound of Mary's salutation. One wonders if there was not some kind of a spiritual witness or communication involved.

Birth itself is a traumatic physical experience. Should this be coupled with associated feelings of parental indifference or even hostility because the baby was not wanted, it is into a rather harsh and loveless world indeed that the little infant comes. Babies were born to be loved, and studies have shown that where love is lacking, there can be serious consequences related to physical development. One wonders if there might not be a corresponding deficiency at the level of personality. What deep scars might be set at such an early age in life!

Wanted: to Be Wanted

I counseled with a woman in her early fifties who was facing a crisis in her life. Her children had all left home, and her husband had moved into a new business venture which was demanding long hours for them both. Some of the children worked with their father in the new business. The mother was the more aggressive parent and had assumed the spiritual leadership in the home in the past, since her husband had felt inadequate and reluctant in this area. Their grown children were reacting to her authority by action and comments related to the joint business venture. Her husband did little to correct the situation. Therefore, what should have been a time of freedom and new interests had become an occasion of fear, frustration, uncertainty, and resentment.

The woman informed me that she had been born very late in the life of her parents. Her father had died when she was thirteen, and her mother—during times of stress and irritation—had reminded her over and over again that she had not been wanted in the first place. The cruel remark had cut deep, creating a wound which was easily reopened during times of stress.

People respond to such inner hurts in different ways. Some become withdrawn and passive, filled with feelings of inferiority and self-pity. Others become authoritative and endeavor to command by aggressive means the love, respect, and security which they need so desperately within. How very much the "little girl" that still lived within the heart of this mother *wanted to be wanted!*

What a privilege it was to assure her that there *was* Someone who really wanted her—Someone who waited with great expectation for her arrival into this world, for she had been hidden in His heart from all eternity past. That Someone was her Heavenly Father. His great desire was for her to be a daughter in His glorious family of love—a love which was proven by the death and resurrection of her Elder Brother, the Lord Jesus Himself.

For all those who feel unloved and unwanted, listen to these encouraging words from the inspired pen of the apostle Paul:

> Long ago, even before he made the world, God chose *you* to be his very own, through what Christ would do for *you;* he decided then to make *you* holy in his eyes, without a single fault—*you* who stand before him covered with his love. His unchanging plan has always

been to adopt *you* into his own family by sending Jesus to die for *you*. And he did this because he *wanted* to! (Eph. 1:4–5 TLB, italics and second-person usage mine).

Fortunately there was further opportunity to share with the woman and her husband. Some of his deeper needs were also seen, and in God's loving grace, both he and his wife were brought to a time of inner healing and reconciliation. They joyfully and tearfully embraced, and the Holy Spirit sealed His ministry by giving them the beautiful blessing of worshiping together for the first time in a heavenly tongue of praise. They left, hand in hand, united in God's healing love for each other and their family.

Suffer the Little Children

It has been said that most of the basic personality traits are pretty well established by eighteen months. These traits would continue to be reinforced and elaborated on throughout the preschool period. Obviously, deficiencies in love or traumatic experiences during these formative years could produce consequences which would carry over into adulthood.

Following a talk on inner healing, God moved most graciously throughout the entire audience. One woman later confided to me that she heard a small inner voice crying out, "Mamma doesn't love me, and Daddy died because he didn't want to be around me anymore!" By facing her past with Jesus, she saw her mother loving and embracing her; at the same time she heard God say He had taken her daddy home to be with Him and that her father loved her with all his heart.

Some may feel such imaginative patterns are rather childish, but this is often the very level where healing needs to occur. It is hard to depreciate the testimony of those who confess they have been healed of hurts that have plagued their inner thought and heart life for years. Jesus indicated that the powerful, profound things of the Kingdom were for those who first were simple and childlike (not childish) in their faith (Matt. 18:2–4).

God's Children: All First-Class Citizens

On another occasion, a very kindly and soft-spoken gentleman told me that while he found some satisfaction in trying to give God's love to others, he had a difficult time in receiving love from others. "In fact," he confided, "I am pretty much disappointed in life. I just seem to be a second-class citizen all the way around." He felt his conversion and Spirit-Baptism experiences hadn't really been first-rate, since they had not appeared to be as sensational as some. In fact, he occasionally doubted his entire Christian experience.

As we counseled together in the Lord, the Holy Spirit reminded him of a traumatic experience he had when he was about three years of age. He had answered the front doorbell and was shocked by the unexpected presence of a large stranger of a different race. Someone in the household, seeing his surprise, had laughingly taunted him with the thought that *they* had come to take him away. At that moment, the idea of possibly not really belonging to the family as a first-class and much-loved member was planted deep within his soul. He had lived for years with a subconscious fear that as a second-class person, he couldn't face the door of the future with confidence, but only with an anxious concern that *they* might be there—to take him away from everything that speaks of love and security.

Even as we spoke, he suddenly burst into tears—something he hadn't been able to do in years. In honestly opening up to me, he also was opening up to the love and truth of the Lord. We recognized that in his adult mind he knew there was nothing in that childhood experience that posed any threat at all to his present welfare—but the little boy within was still unsure. Again we re-lived the scene, this time with Jesus by his side. He could face both the door and the stranger, secure in the protection and love of his Elder Brother. Furthermore, the love of Jesus is an extension of the love of our Heavenly Father—and in His family, everybody is a first-class citizen.

The Horns of a Childhood Dilemma

The following story is an example of how the Lord will arrange situations to assure us of His personal concern that our spirit be set free. The woman who sat across from me in the eighteenth-century drawing room of the old retreat house had just made an unusual remark: "I find I have a deep resentment toward my mother. She is seeking the Baptism in the Holy Spirit, but to be perfectly honest, I hope she doesn't receive it!" She went on to indicate that she was happy in her home and with her family—as long as mother was not around. It was like being changed into another person whenever her mother came to visit. She just couldn't be herself, and consequently she just withdrew. In her mother's presence she felt restrained, intimidated, frustrated, and resentful.

We shared rather generally for a time, trusting the Holy Spirit to give the wisdom and discernment needed for an honest, sincere, but very distraught sister in the Lord. Suddenly she looked at the chair I was seated in and exclaimed, "Why that chair, and even the pattern in the pillow, is almost identical to the one in which my grandfather died when I was just a little girl." With that, the problem began to unravel. She had loved her grandfather very much. His unexpected death had apparently set in her mind a fear that someone you love might suddenly be taken from you. As a reaction, she gravitated toward the one person in her family who could supply the strength and security she needed. Her father was weak, so she sought her mother, a rather authoritative and domineering person.

Her earlier dependence brought her to a place of great frustration during her teenage years. She needed the support of her mother, but her mother's dominating ways stifled her developing personality. This had all been rather sharply focused by a dream she had just before the retreat. She saw herself as a teenager greatly distressed because her mother had chosen to wear some of her clothes, and she didn't want to be that closely identified with her.

As we continued our time of counseling, it became apparent that she had been placed on the horns of a dilemma. As a young girl, she needed the strength and security her mother could provide, but she also wanted the privilege of becoming a person in her own right. Her mother's overbearing behavior created a keen inner conflict which had never been healed. We saw that in Jesus she could find the security and freedom that she wanted. It was also pointed out that her mother undoubtedly had some rather deep needs in her own life that had never been resolved. Her dominating conduct may well have been her unfruitful attempt to find a place of respect and appreciation.

It was now possible to review the past scenes in her life with a sense of Christ's forgiveness toward her mother, at the same time confessing her need of forgiveness as well. The Holy Spirit had revealed the root of her problem and assured her of His forgiving and redeeming power in Christ Jesus. While resentful feelings might occasionally surge up, she was now in control of the problem. His love could bring an answer for all concerned. Truth that sets us free can keep us free, when confessed in the power of God's releasing Spirit.

Understanding Others and Ourselves

Sometimes the Lord wants us to gain insight into the needs of others who may be closely involved in our own problems. Understanding them helps us to understand ourselves, and appropriate God's forgiveness. A teenage girl approached us at the close of a meeting and requested prayer that she might have a more harmonious relationship with her parents. She had just recently made a genuine commitment to Christ and sincerely wanted His love to fill her life and heal a strained relationship with her family. She and her father had tried to discuss their problems, with little success, and visits home from her school usually developed into rather unpleasant affairs in spite of basic good intentions.

I inquired if she had ever experienced a time of emotional shock when she was a little girl. Almost immediately she recalled a particularly painful episode when she was nine years old. Her parents were missionaries and had decided to send her and her older sister to boarding school before their return to the mission field. They postponed informing her of their decision until the day of her departure. She was utterly stunned and became almost hysterical when she realized what was going to happen. She was deeply hurt that they had not even consulted her beforehand. The hurt in her heart festered into resentment and finally broke forth in years of outright rebellion. Even after giving her life to Jesus and being filled with the Holy Spirit, she needed a deep, inner healing. God had graciously drawn her to Himself, and filled her life with His Spirit that she might be completely set free.

Her father had spoken many times of his own disappointing childhood, and she had detected some bitterness relative to his early family life. Often distorted family relationships carry over into our fellowship with our Heavenly Father. I inquired if she felt her father had served the Lord basically from a sense of freedom or fear—as a labor of love or duty. She admitted there were elements of fear and obligation involved; to cross God's will could well invoke His wrath and displeasure. If such indeed had been the case, she came to see that that day of decision was also something most painful for her father. Whatever direction he took, he knew he was going to displease someone—either his daughter or God. Within that context, there did not seem to be an alternative. For the first time, she began to appreciate some of the agony of soul her father had experienced on that tragic occasion. And he had to hold all of his feelings within!

We then pictured the departure scene, but this time we saw Jesus comforting His little sister and ministering His grace to her bewildered and grieving parents. He wanted very much to bring healing to them all. In this light, God began to melt her heart, and she expressed forgiveness toward her parents. She then asked the Lord to forgive her for her unlovely and selfish reactions, which had inflicted pain upon her family. In her spirit, she sought their forgiveness as well, and claimed the love of God for whatever inner healing was yet needed by her parents.

Love and respect are basic needs for us all, but only the Holy Spirit Himself can undo some of the tangled threads of our lives. It was a tearful but thankful young woman who that night allowed the Holy Spirit to intercede through her on behalf of her needs, and those of the family. One of the ministries of our Blessed Comforter is to wash and heal the inner man by means of spiritual prayer and song. Together we rejoiced in the Spirit for a glorious healing. There undoubtedly would still be some trying times, but we were assured God's love and truth would prevail.

Soul Poisons: Resentment and Self-Pity

Resentment and self-pity are potent poisons for the soul. Both can darken and deaden our spiritual relationship with

God and others. I recall a tragic story from the wife of a clergyman who had divorced her, and then re-married into the immediate family. This grieving sister in the Lord then had to look to her own resources for her support. It was a rather sordid affair, which she had to face continually or suffer estrangement from her children and grandchildren. The entire situation was most cruel and complicated. God had graciously provided strength and courage, but the wound went from surface to center and was continually being reinfected both from circumstances without and attitudes within.

Several times she mentioned that if she lived a thousand years she could never forget the injustice inflicted upon her. There were definite indications of resentment and self-pity. How could these be faced without worsening a bad situation? The Lord brought a word of wisdom. In the natural, it was indeed a most cruelly unjust situation—a pitiful plight if there ever was one. But the Lord warned that as justified as she might be in the natural for resentment and self pity, these were the poisons by which Satan would sicken her soul in a tormenting fashion. God had given her the antidote—forgiveness and compassion—but she must remain faithful to the prescription or she could well lose more than just her peace of mind—the Enemy had found the toxic materials for a total breakdown.

She recognized this and confessed her desire to remain true to God's word for her life. Then together we confessed her liberty as a daughter of the King—a handmaiden whom God could use in mending other hearts which had been shattered by similar tragedy. How wonderful it was to bring Jesus onto the scene, for He can become a Husband to those who sorrow, and a Provider for those in great spiritual need. Together we confessed divine restoration for her soul and claimed for her a future filled with God's grace, both directly and through her brothers and sisters in Christ. She left with a desire to share more of the Lord's love in her current school situation where there were many spiritual sons and daughters who needed a true "mother in Israel."

Jesus: a Model Brother and Husband

God's order for our lives and homes is always fair, but occasionally past experiences can make it appear unjust, and lead to sharp conflicts within. A sincere and devout woman once approached me in deep distress, which she confessed was bringing her close to a breaking point. She had recognized the need for her husband, whom she loved, to truly be not only the head of her home, but the lord of her life, in the loving, responsible, divine sense of the word. (See the chapter on "The Spirit-Filled Home" in the author's book, *Overflowing Life*.) However, such a place of spiritual submission caused a surge of inner resentment bordering on rebellion. She wanted to relate to divine order, but just couldn't bring herself to it. "It isn't fair, it just isn't fair!" she exclaimed over and over again.

A look into her early childhood years revealed the reason for her intense feelings. She was the middle daughter between two brothers who were favored as the eldest and the youngest in the family. To further aggravate the situation, there was an aunt who very obviously preferred the two boys. As a result, a deep-rooted male antagonism developed which she could not resolve. We began discussing the baptizing power of God's Spirit which she had already experienced. There was to be a releasing stream for her which could wash away the resentment and pain of her childhood. By allowing the Holy Spirit to bring the Lord Jesus into her problem as her Elder Brother, she was no longer in the middle of a threesome. Furthermore, He would always treat her with kindness and respect as his much-loved little sister. He would make her feel like the princess she was—a daughter of the King. The Lord also is the model after which all husbands are to follow. This kind of lordship provides the protection and loving encouragement which allows a wife to reach her full potential as a person and as a handmaiden of God. Here was the truth that was needed to set her free. God's Spirit was the healing balm that ministered that truth to her scarred soul. That truth was centered in Jesus—for only He can release us from the prisons (and persons) of our past.

Conditioned Reflexes

Conditioned (learned) reflexes were mentioned in an earlier chapter, using Pavlov's dog as an example. Pavlov, you recall, rang a bell at every feeding for the dog. The dog was finally conditioned to salivate by the bell alone, whether food was present or not.

We all have been conditioned to some degree by a variety of different kinds of food-bell situations encountered in the past. We may not even be aware the reflex has been established, but are bewildered by the intensity of our emotional reactions to certain situations.

One woman gave me a vivid illustration of this from her own life. She and her husband had been baptized in the Holy Spirit and were enjoying the freedom of worship and sharing which are associated with home prayer meetings. She noticed, however, that if anyone shed tears—whether they were of sadness, joy, or whatever—she was repulsed to the point of nausea. She couldn't understand why such tender scenes should be so revolting to her. Her emotional response was way out of proportion.

After she engaged in serious and prayerful reflection, the Lord reminded her of a crucial period in her early adolescence. Her mother was an alcoholic whom her father despised. He would occasionally call home to inquire if she had gotten drunk again. Her mother would endeavor to force her to lie to her father concerning her intoxicated condition by using tears of self-pity. She recalled she didn't want to be deceitful, but couldn't tolerate the deplorable scene of her mother crying and sobbing to avoid her husband's scorn. Before long, she subconsciously began to associate tears with contemptible situations which evoke painful inner conflicts.

Realizing the truth is the first step to freedom, if we are walking in the healing light of God's Holy Spirit. This woman's release from the past was progressive. Once she understood the cause of her conditioned reflex, she was able to review the past with the loving, forgiving Spirit of Jesus. She also possessed the truth and the power necessary to effectively resist the occasional surges of emotion which sometimes catch us offguard in provocative situations. The reflex pattern can be broken. Sometimes God does it instantaneously, but many times He desires our cooperation, for in the process of faith and obedience we mature in our Christian character.

Accepted as We Are

After I had shared along the lines of inner healing in a recent meeting, a very timid man and his wife waited for an opportunity to discuss some of his needs. (I usually share some of my own past hang-ups in such talks, for I have found it is much easier for all of us to talk to people who, we feel, understand us, and have experienced similar problems themselves.)

The man was the youngest member in a family of seven. Throughout all of his boyhood days, he had been bullied, dominated, and deprecated. He reacted to such humiliation and ridicule by endeavoring to excel in his schooling and subsequent work and thereby prove himself in the eyes of others. Even in his Christian experience, he felt he was a failure, no matter how hard he tried. He had enrolled in a witnessing clinic, hoping that their techniques might bring him a sense of confidence and perhaps a measure of success by their standards of achievement. Actually, their aggressive methods only aggravated his feelings of inferiority. Even in his areas of achievement, he had the uneasy feeling that people might respect what he had done more than they appreciated him as a person. So deep was the sense of failure in every area of his life, that he couldn't even look people in the eye. (The whole time he was talking, he kept his eyes on the floor.)

I shared with him some of my own feelings along these lines as a boy and how even now new situations cause me to lean hard on the Lord, but I had discovered He was always there. What a joy it was to assure him that Jesus always accepts us as we are, and by the power of His Spirit progressively transforms us into His own image—if we will accept His grace without trying to add our effort to it. All God wants us to be is ourselves as He has uniquely made us. But we can only be ourselves as we find ourselves in Christ Jesus; and it is the Holy Spirit who puts and keeps us there.

As we talked together, he began to relax and respond to God's love for him as a respected son. It was possible then to review the painful parts of his past and confess God's forgiveness for all who, in trying to establish their own identities, had almost destroyed his. We pictured Jesus as a Loving Brother by his side all during his boyhood years. Never once would his Big Brother ever ridicule or humiliate him before others. Always, even during times of correction, there would be an abiding attitude of encouragement, and full appreciation for him as a person.

Before long, I noticed he was looking me in the eye, and again I was aware of witnessing a sunrise of the soul. I am moved within even as I write, for I have an inner conviction that someone is going to read these words who needs to know that God loves, accepts, and appreciates them as they are. This is the ground from which progress in Christ Jesus can be made by His grace and through the power of God's Holy Spirit. God loves you more than you will ever know—He loves you! That is the only basis by which we can follow the Lord in faith and obedience. If you first look up into the loving eyes of your Heavenly Father, you will be able to share that love when looking into the eyes of your fellowmen.

Two Basic Needs: Love and Respect

We were seated in the lobby of the conference hotel. A woman in her early fifties was speaking in a rather soft-spoken way, but the heart-cry behind every word was loud and clear. Her life had been a series of seeming failures, one after another. This negative attitude had been repeatedly reinforced by a dominating mother, ever since she could remember. Never had she been able to please her mother and receive the *love* and *respect* she so desperately needed. She tried all kinds of things to gain the approval and acceptance of her classmates. "I used to volunteer to be the turner for skip rope at school, just to be wanted by the others girls, who would all take their turns jumping while I held the rope!"

She related how she was slow in dressing on one occasion and honestly didn't realize her mother was impatiently waiting. Finally her mother flew into her room and furiously berated her for her slowness and stupidity. In a fit of anger, she clutched at the arm of her child with such force her fingernails drew blood from her arm. Even on her deathbed, all the mother could talk about was her daughter's many failures. After the death of both of her parents, she felt guilty for not visiting her mother's grave as often as she did that of her father.

She also vividly recalled a piano recital as a little girl where, panicked by fear, she was unable to complete her part of the program. Even as an adult, somewhat accomplished in her music, she found great difficulty in playing the piano at church. Doubts and fears carried over into other areas of her life, and there had been times when she wasn't even sure of her salvation. She had been prayed for to receive the Baptism in the Holy Spirit, but doubted whether she had really received, and questioned the reality of her heavenly tongue of praise.

I assured her I knew how she felt, for I had suffered through many humiliating experiences similar to hers—including a rather traumatic piano recital. I encouraged her that if the Lord could reach me, He could also help her. I could see hope begin to rise in her heart. God's love has a way of stirring up hope which can mature into an active faith.

I recall a similar story from the lips of an accomplished musician who had acquired a confidence in her artistic specialty, but who felt most insecure in areas of human relationships. Basically, she was a warm, affectionate person who wanted and needed to be accepted and appreciated for herself—not just her music.

Her father was a religious disciplinarian who showed little love or affection for her apart from her gift of music, which he encouraged. As a result, she came to feel people wanted her only for her talent and the way it might enhance their program. After being deeply hurt on a number of occasions, she began to withdraw from any kind of close relationship with people—an attitude which some interpreted as a professional aloofness. Actually, it was a defense against the pain of possible personal rejection. It is very difficult to give love or receive love when we feel it is necessary to maintain protective barriers.

In both of the above situations, it was the love of God translated into life through the personal testimonies of others which spoke assurance to two who had been grievously wounded during childhood. I have discovered that sharing similar experiences of my own and others with those who need help makes them realize they are not alone in their problem, and the Lord is just as ready and willing to heal them as He has many others who have undergone the same kinds of deep distress.

The Healing Power of Forgiveness

Many times we have mentioned in the foregoing testimonies the importance of forgiveness in receiving the healing of our soul. The forgiveness may involve ourselves or others as the following two stories illustrate. The first involves a young man who was plagued with self-condemnation and guilt. A beloved aunt was in the hospital, and he planned to visit her, since her illness had become rather serious. However, on his way, he stopped at a bar for a drink. One led to another, until he was in no condition to make the hospital visit, and the opportunity was lost—forever—because the aunt died before he saw her again. He later made a genuine commitment to the Lord and earnestly sought His forgiveness, but the past incident of personal failure continued to haunt his life.

It does little good to tell someone with such inner hurt that God has forgiven them and that they should forget the whole thing. They already know that in their head; it is their heart that must be informed. We began by honestly confessing we can't work up a sense of forgiveness in our minds. The Holy Spirit must accomplish this within our spirit; then our hearts and minds can accept the truth. Again, the Holy Spirit helps us at the level of true heart-understanding by enabling us to relive the situation with Jesus. Since the spiritual realm is outside the limitations of time, not every missed opportunity is a total loss.

I suggested the young man picture himself re-visiting the hospital scene with the Lord and asking his aunt to forgive him for his failure. He could assure her that he had received forgiveness from God, but he wanted everything right with her as well. Certainly if in some way the situation had been

reversed and he were the one approached by her for forgiveness, he would quickly and joyfully extend it. In like
fashion, then, he was going to readily and joyfully receive her
forgiveness, and with that, forgive himself. The spirit of
forgiveness prompted by Christ's love is altogether sufficient to
cover any situation. In the name of Jesus and on the authority
of God's Word, we then confessed that he was released—spirit,
soul, and body. And he was!

The Holy Spirit has a way of bringing a lightness of soul
and spirit within. One woman suggested to me, after a similar
prayer for release, that it was like the clean, cool feeling which
one senses after eating peppermint candy. I knew what she
was talking about.

The second situation involved a woman who requested
prayer concerning a persistent desire to overeat. I felt this was
a symptom of something deeper and suggested we recognize
the searching streams of God's Spirit which can bring release
and healing to our innermost needs. In our prayer and counsel
we then covered some of the areas in the overcoming-evil-with
good list discussed earlier. The theme of resentment persisted
in my mind, and I finally inquired if there was anyone against
whom she was resentful. She acted as if she had been slapped,
and finally, in obvious distress, she confessed that her husband
had divorced her and remarried another woman after their
children had grown and left home. She was very bitter, and in
her heart was an awful emptiness that natural food could
never satisfy. Her children, who were Spirit-filled Christians,
had tried to caution her concerning the devastating power of
resentment, but she had interpreted this as their taking sides
with their father against her.

Only God's forgiveness going *to* and *from* her life could heal
her soul. This involved asking the Lord to forgive her for her
unlovely thoughts toward her children and former husband.
Then in God's grace and by the power of His Spirit, she was to

forgive her former husband for whatever injustice he may have
inflicted upon her—even to the point of informing God that in
the day of judgment she would not require any kind of
retaliation in the name of justice. (How often we say we
forgive, but comfort ourselves with the sense of soulish
satisfaction we will receive when they get what's coming to
them in that final day of reckoning.) The "Father, forgive
them" attitude can only be a work of God's Spirit within, for
man cannot work up that kind of forgiveness. Finally, the
inner attitude of forgiveness would involve some necessary
restitution in this situation, since sharp words and actions had
reached other lives.

It was a serious time of prayer which followed, but we
claimed the inner power of the Holy Spirit and His intercessory ministry through our heavenly tongue of praise. There is
a purifying and healing power to praise which is most needed
in times of deep depression. True worship confesses the
greatness of God's grace in forgiving our sins and fills us with
enough love to share that forgiveness with others as well.
There is perhaps no greater expression of God's love through
our lives than the spirit of forgiveness.

Adhesions and All

I would like to conclude this chapter with a personal
experience. My father died when I was three, and in spite of
the loving care of my godly mother, I developed a full-blown
inferiority complex. It became sufficiently acute that I
couldn't even read aloud in class or participate in any kind of
an oral presentation. I dreaded Monday mornings and the
threat of embarrassment and humiliation which school always
presented. Obviously I had to overcome some of this as I
proceeded with my higher education, but many hangovers
remained. It was my inability to pray aloud or present any
kind of a public witness that finally drove me to Jesus for the

baptizing power of His Spirit. This was after I had obtained my doctoral degree and had established a home and a family.

The Lord and I are still working on some things, but a measure of progress has been made. Most of it has come in steps and stages. Some time ago, I was invited to participate as a speaker at a family retreat for a week. I arrived alone, and went through the usual confusion of registration and finally checking out my cabin. About that time, a bell began to ring, and the campers started lining up at one of the buildings which I assumed was the dining hall.

In other meetings, the leaders ate together to conserve conference time, but in the rush of registration, no instruction had been given to me. I remember wishing that my wife was along for company, since nearly everyone was a stranger to me. With a familiar feeling of resignation, I recall thinking, "If this isn't the story of my life—always on the *outside* looking *in!*" However, I joined the lunch line, and began visiting with the other campers. The meal was a grand time of fellowship with new friends, and I forgot all about my initial feeling of distress—but God didn't.

Later in the week, I had to leave for one day because of a prior commitment; consequently, I missed the counselors' meeting in which they decided to save the front rows of seats for the young people during the evening meeting. I arrived back in camp in time for the evening meeting, and after debating where to sit, I forwent my back-seat preference for a seat on the front row. Two basic reasons prompted my decision: I wanted to support the speaker by my presence and prayer; and I wanted to be available to counsel those who might come forward for prayer following the message of the evening.

As the starting time approached, I noticed I was the only hairless-headed person on the front row, but didn't give it much thought. Then it happened! One of the camp leaders came to the microphone and clearly and loudly informed everyone that we were to remember the earlier announcement concerning the front seats for the young people—a category to which I rather obviously did not belong. I tried to act nonchalant, but a beet red blush betrayed my inner embarrassment. I was sure everyone's eye was focused in my direction, and the coming of the Lord would have been a welcome escape. I recovered my composure with the comforting thought that my motives were clear before God, regardless of what the speaker thought. Therefore, I had every right to remain where I was. The comfort was rather fleeting, however, for I immediately recalled the emphasis on obedience which had been set before the young people. What kind of example would I be if I stubbornly remained where I was?

There was no alternative; I would have to arise and make my way to the side exit in front of the whole congregation. I decided I would wait about a half a minute, then casually stroll to the door as if heading for a drink of water, which I didn't need. If all of this sounds very foolish and self-centered, it is—but you have to have had a particular kind of background to fully appreciate how agonizing such foolish reactions (conditioned reflexes?) can really be. Anyway, I found a place in the back, cooled off, calmed down, and enjoyed the rest of the service including prayer and counseling with others afterward. I had already forgotten the humiliating incident earlier in the service—but God hadn't.

During the course of the week, an interesting testimony was related to me by a friend. It concerned a woman who was very timid and withdrawn. A spiritual counselor, while visiting with her, was given an unusual mental picture by the Lord. She saw a ring of little girls all gaily playing ring-around-a-rosy. Outside of this happy circle, she saw a lonely, unloved little girl looking on rather wistfully. The counselor shared this with the woman and asked if it meant anything to her. She immediately responded by bursting into tears and exclaiming, "Yes, that is the story of my life—I have always been on the outside looking in!"

She was encouraged to review the entire scene again, but this time she was to see Jesus put His loving arms around His lonely little sister and introduce her into the circle of the other little girls. Now she had one hand in His and the other in the hand of a newfound playmate. So warm was His love that she found she could forgive her little friends for any thoughtless behavior which may have excluded her from their play. Furthermore, she could ask them to forgive her for any unfriendly attitudes and defenses which may have caused them to feel she didn't really want to be with them anyway. The circle of love and forgiveness was complete—all because Jesus had been brought into the picture.

It was a beautiful and meaningful story, but I didn't give it much personal attention until the next morning when I awakened early to pray. I recalled the lovely scene, and as I did, the Lord informed me there was something in it for me personally. "Oh," I replied, "is that so?" "Yes," the Lord responded. "Do you remember the lunch-time incident when you first arrived?" "Well, yes, I guess I do. I was feeling rather lonely and leftout." "Do you also remember the front-row incident of the other evening?" I replied emphatically, "I'll never forget it!"

The Holy Spirit then reminded me of an incident in my life when I was about twelve and in the midst of my inferiority problem at school. A boy who lived across the street had developed a great dislike for me, even though we had previously been very close friends. He took every opportunity to humiliate and ridicule me before my classmates. One Saturday morning, twelve of us were going to a baseball game together. While we were waiting on the corner for the bus, he said, "Let's see if everybody is here." With that, he counted everyone but me, and loudly proclaimed, "Yes, all eleven of us are here." Someone mentioned he must have made a mistake, because they had counted twelve. Whereupon he very carefully counted again—one by one, excluding me a second time. Someone then remarked, "But you didn't count Frost." "Oh, well," he promptly replied, "Frost doesn't count anyway!"

The Lord showed me that while I had long-since forgiven the young boy in my heart, and any festering resentment had been removed, some adhesive scar tissue had remained in the form of reflex attitudes. The same thing can occur in a surgical situation. An inflamed appendix can be removed, and the source of infection is gone, but adhesions can develop which restrict the inner freedom of movement. Sometimes we, too, can truly forgive, but still need to be released from leftover adhesions in the form of negative, self-centered predispositions. I had a hangover from childhood of feeling little, lonely, and left out when in a group where I was not sure of my position. The Lord concluded our little counseling session rather simply, but clearly: "As long as you are feeling lonely and unloved within, how can I use you to help others who may likewise be standing around feeling little, lonely, and left-out?" I saw the truth of it and immediately sensed a warm, inner release in my spirit for which I profusely praised God.

The Lord then suggested I might want to share my insight in the morning teaching session. "Oh," I replied, "do You mean the whole thing?" Whereupon the Spirit made it clear that that was the idea all right. I tried to argue with the Lord that it might not go over as well as He thought. He simply responded, "Why don't you try it and see? You have nothing to lose but your pride." It was a persuasive answer, so I decided I would—and the response was both immediate and amazing.

I was approached by all kinds of people throughout the remaining days of the camp. Young people, old people—even counselors and directors—opened their hearts for spiritual healing. I realized then how many people go throughout large portions of their lives with hidden hurts to which they have finally resigned themselves. All hope is gone, and they are serving God as best they know how, in spite of unresolved conflicts and great spiritual needs for release and inner healing. The story is the same wherever I have gone. It involves leaders as well as others. Little do we sometimes surmise what is behind the platform smile and professional decorum. How very much God wants to set His people free. That is the whole purpose of this little book.

8

THE ONCOMING
AND UPON-FALLING
A Mantle of Power

And the Spirit of the Lord shall rest *upon* him, the Spirit of wisdom, understanding, counsel and might; the Spirit of knowledge and of the fear of the Lord. His delight will be obedience to the Lord. He will not *judge* by appearance, false evidence, or hearsay, but will defend the poor and the exploited. He will *rule* against the wicked who oppress them. For he will be *clothed* with fairness and with truth. (Isa. 11:2–5 TLB, italics mine)

Behold My Servant, Whom I uphold; My elect, in Whom My soul delights! I have put My Spirit *upon* Him; He will bring forth *justice* and right, and reveal truth to the nations. . . . He will bring forth *justice* in truth. (Isa. 42:1, 3 TAB, italics mine)

The Spirit of the Lord God is *upon* me, because the Lord has anointed me to bring good news to the suffering and afflicted. He has sent me to comfort the broken-hearted, to announce *liberty* to captives and to open the eyes of the blind . . . For I, the Lord, love *justice.* (Isa. 61:1, 8 TLB, italics mine)

And the Holy Spirit descended *upon* Him in bodily form, like a dove, and a voice came from heaven saying, You are my beloved *Son* in whom I am well pleased. . . . Then Jesus went back full of and under the *power* of the Holy Spirit to Galilee. . . . And they were amazed at His teaching, for His word was with *authority* and

154

power. . . . With *authority* and *power* He commands the foul spirits, and they come out! (Luke 3:22; 4:1,14,36 various versions)

God anointed Jesus of Nazareth with the Holy Ghost and with *power*: who went about doing good, and healing all that were oppressed of the devil; for God was with him. (Acts 10:38, italics mine)

And Jesus came and spake unto them saying, All *power* [authority] is given unto me in heaven and in earth. (Matt. 28:18)

Behold, I give unto you *power* [authority] to tread on serpents and scorpions, and over all the power of the enemy: and nothing shall by any means hurt you. (Luke 10:19)

As the Father has sent me, even so send I you. And when He had said this, He breathed on them and said, Receive the Holy Spirit. . . . And, behold, I send forth the promise of my Father *upon* you: but tarry in the city of Jerusalem until you are *clothed* with *power* from on high, for you shall receive *power* after that the Holy Spirit has come *upon* you! (John 20:21-22; Luke 24:49; Acts 1:8, various versions)

And when the day of Pentecost was fully come, they were all of one accord in one place. And suddenly there came a sound from heaven as of a rushing *mighty* wind . . . and there appeared unto them cloven tongues like as of fire, and it sat *upon* each of them. And they were all filled with the Holy Ghost, and began to speak with other tongues as the Spirit gave them utterance. (Acts 2:1-4)

And as I [Peter] began to speak, the Holy Ghost fell *on* them [Gentiles], as on us at the beginning. (Acts 11:15)

THE MANTLE OF AUTHORITY

There is a significant theme that threads its way through the above Scriptures. The little word "upon" when associated with the Holy Spirit rather consistently speaks of the *power, authority,* and *government* of God. Divine dominion is always related to justice and liberty, that God's wise and loving purpose might be manifested throughout all of His creation. In other words, the Holy Spirit is to rest as a mantle of authority *upon the shoulders* of those who are called (commissioned) according to His purpose. The "shoulder" in Scripture often refers to divine *responsibility* and *authority*:

> And the government shall be *upon* his *shoulder*. . . . His ever-expanding, peaceful *government* will never end. He will *rule* with perfect fairness and justice. (Isa. 9:6–7 TLB, italics mine)

> And I will *clothe* him with thy robe, and strengthen him with thy girdle, and I will commit thy *government* into his hand . . . And the key of the house of David (authority) will I lay *upon his shoulder* . . . And they shall hang *upon* him the honor and full weight of *responsibility* for his father's house. (Isa. 22:21–22,24 various versions)

The two passages above, concerning the Messiah and Eliakim (prefect in the palace of King Hezekiah) respectively, refer to the custom of wearing the ensign of office upon the shoulder. The same idea is expressed by the epaulets worn by military officers. Likewise, royal robes and stately clothing traditionally have been associated with recognized authority and responsibility.

There is a sense in which Adam and Eve had been divinely clothed with a *mantle of authority* when they were commissioned by God to reign over all of creation—land, sea, and air.

> Let us make mankind in Our image, after Our likeness; and let them have *dominion* (*rule, complete authority*) over the fish of the *sea,* the birds of the *air,* the beasts and over all of the *earth.* . . . So God created man in His own image . . . male and female created He them. And God blessed them, and said to them, Be fruitful, multiply, and fill the earth and *subdue* it, and take *dominion* (*mastery*) over every living creature. (Gen. 1:26–28 various versions)

The first man and woman were to be far more than glorified

gardeners and keepers of a newly created zoo: their destiny involved subjecting all of creation to God's holy purpose—that it might become the setting in which a family of royal sons and daughters would forever express the wonderful life of God's pattern Son, the Lord Jesus Christ.

It was through Christ as God's "Second Adam" that Satan was stripped of his legal right to rule. The triumph of the cross established the Lordship of our Christ, to whom all power and authority was given, both in heaven and on earth. Satan at this present point in history is a usurper of the throne who only can exercise his authority over those who submit to his rule. Our position in Christ has freed us from the penalty and power of sin. Eventually, even the cursed creation will experience a restoration of God's original purpose as His kingdom is established on earth as it is in heaven. The return of Jesus Christ as King of kings and Lord of lords will restore divine purpose as it was originally planned. We have a responsibility in assuming the authority which is ours in preparing the way for the coming of our King—perhaps even in hastening the day of His appearing. The preparation is twofold: it involves a unity of love and truth *within* God's people, and a witness of love and truth *without* to a world that needs to know that Jesus is Lord.

Without the mantle of God's Holy Spirit, we are powerless to perform the will of God on earth as it is in heaven. Jesus Christ is the Head of His Body. As our Head, He rules and reigns in the heavenlies; as members of His Body, we are to rule and reign over principalities and powers here on earth through the power of His Holy Spirit. Only by God's Spirit can God's end-time purpose on earth be accomplished through His people. His end-time purpose will prepare the way for Christ's return and the fulfillment of the Father's desire for a royal family that will rule and reign in love forever.

GOD'S PATTERN SON

The pattern for realizing God's purpose in a kingdom-family has been set for us by our Kingly Brother, the Lord Jesus. "As the Father has sent me, so send I you," were the words of our Lord as He commissioned His disciples to proclaim the Good News of the Kingdom. The pattern of His life becomes a blueprint for ours as well. Jesus was born by the Spirit into an earthly family. We likewise must be born by the Spirit into God's heavenly family. As a child, Jesus increased in wisdom and stature and in favor with God and man. In other words, He developed as a whole person—spiritually, mentally, physically, and socially. His boyhood years were in preparation for the privileges and responsibilities of mature sonship. His character was proven and perfected (developed) that He might shoulder the divine task for which He came into this world. None of us can bypass the time and testing which is necessary to perfect our characters that we, too, may complete the divine purpose for which we have been placed in God's Kingdom Family.

Jesus was *born* as a child in Bethlehem, but He was *recognized* as a Son at His baptism in the Jordan River. The Father, Himself, made the proclamation, "Thou art my beloved Son in whom I am well pleased." Immediately, the Holy Spirit descended upon Him in bodily form like a dove. I have always pictured the dove in my mind as alighting upon his right *shoulder,* as if symbolizing the mantle of God's Spirit which *invested* Him with the power and authority to carry out His divine commission as God's Son and the Savior of the world. With the coming of the Holy Spirit upon Him, Jesus entered into a new order and realm of temptation. The higher level of authority and responsibility which mature sonship brings always involves new levels of testing and temptation as well.

The temptations of the Spirit-filled Christ are worth the careful study of every Spirit-filled Christian. (This theme is more fully developed in the two chapters on temptation and testing which are included in the second edition of the author's book, *Overflowing Life*.) Jesus wore His mantle well, and proved out the power which God gives by His Spirit for responsible sonship. The Lord Jesus not only frustrated the designs of the devil, but fulfilled the will of the Father. By the Spirit of the living God *upon* His life, and the word of the living God *within* His heart, He became the Model for overcomers of every age. "As many as are led by the Spirit of God, they are the sons of God" (Rom. 8:14). Sonship requires the leadership of God's Spirit.

> And Jesus being full of the Holy Ghost returned from Jordan, and was *led* by the Spirit into the wilderness, being forty days tempted of the devil. . . . And Jesus returned in the *power* of the Spirit into Galilee where He preached the gospel to the poor; healed the broken-hearted; preached deliverance to the captives, and recovery of sight to the blind and set at liberty those who were bruised! (Luke 4:1,14,18 various versions)

The Lord was demonstrating the power of the Kingdom to those who were to become *united* in His life, and eventually become an effective *witness* to the entire world.

LET THY MANTLE FALL ON ME

There is a fascinating story in the Old Testament that very beautifully illustrates the principles of sonship and authority. The occasion is the ascension of Elijah, who had been a spiritual father and example for young Elisha.

The call of God to the prophetic ministry had first come to Elisha unexpectedly while he and his father's plowman were working in the springtime meadows. Elijah, following the instructions of the Lord (I Kings 19:16), suddenly appeared behind Elisha and cast his rough camel's-hair mantle *upon* his shoulder (I Kings 19:19).

Elisha immediately perceived the signficance of this dramatic moment: this was a token of *investiture* with the prophet's office and of *adoption* as a son. Undoubtedly Elisha—a man of God's choosing—had been readied for his call by fulfilling his earthly responsibilities as a son in his father's family. The farm was to Elisha what the carpenter shop was to Jesus—a place of preparation for divine purpose. He apparently was well aware of Elijah's prophetic ministry, and perhaps in his own heart had secretly hoped that some day he might follow in his footsteps, or at least join the school of the prophets. At any rate, he was ready for his appointment.

Elisha quickly responded to his commission by slaying his favorite oxen and preparing their flesh over a fire kindled from the wood of his plow. In the feast that followed, he publicly declared his decision to henceforth be a plowman in the meadows of God's divine purpose—the hearts and lives of his people.

Some ten years of silence elapsed before we again heard of Elisha in the record of Scripture. His time of training under his master was soon to conclude. God had indicated that Elijah would shortly be taken up into heaven by a whirlwind. He visited the schools of the prophets at Bethel and Jericho for the last time. Repeatedly, the sons of the prophets reminded Elisha that he soon was to be separated from his beloved father and master. Filled with sorrow by the anticipated loss, and determined to remain loyally and lovingly by Elijah's side down to the very last moment, he replied, "I know, I know, please speak no more of it!"

Three times over, Elijah suggested Elisha might wish to remain behind, as the path of his life was now measured by but a few remaining steps. But what was there to remain behind for if Elijah was still on the move? It was upon him that the mantle of God's Spirit uniquely rested. To whom else could Elisha have turned? How differently the story might have ended if Elisha had given up in sadness and despair. His reply, however, was clear and determined. "As the Lord liveth, and as thy soul liveth, I will not leave thee" (II Kings 2:2). Could it be his persistence in following Elijah was related to a peculiar awareness of God's presence—the same powerful attraction which drew him to the old prophet in the first place? Was there a hidden hope that something of that presence might remain, and even rest upon his own life after Elijah's departure?

The two men finally approached the Jordan River (a symbol of dedication and decision), and as Elijah struck the waters with his mantle, the power of God's Spirit provided a dry path and led them on. Only a few momentous steps remained before them, and Elijah paused to ask Elisha a question—a question that could not have been asked before, for it was offered only to those who had paid the price of discipleship. "Ask what I shall do for you before I am taken from you" (II Kings 2:9 TAB). Elisha's reply would determine his destiny for the remainder of his days. How tragic if he had requested a professorship in the school of the prophets where he might live out the rest of his life in a well-deserved position of esteem because of his historic relationship with Elijah.

But Elisha's reply was, "I pray thee, let a double portion of thy spirit be *upon* me!" (II Kings 2:9). This was not a presumptuous demand, but a proper request based upon the double-portion privilege which is inherited by an elder son. Elisha was asking that he might inherit the power and authority which was resident in the prophetic mantle of Elijah. He was informed that his desire would be fulfilled if he was present at the moment of Elijah's departure. Then the Scriptures state that the two of them went on talking together, a rough, old saint and his beloved son savoring their last remaining moments of earthly fellowship.

Suddenly there appeared a chariot and horses of fire which parted them, and the fiery old prophet was caught up in a whirlwind. With great intensity of feeling, Elisha cried out, "My father, my father, the chariot of Israel and the horsemen thereof!" (II Kings 2:12), and he saw him no more. Indeed, Elijah had been as a *father* to Elisha and as a *savior* to Israel; now he was gone. Surely Elisha stood in stunned silence for a few moments. Then, slowly, the present world came into focus, and his eyes fell upon a familiar object lying at his feet—an old, well-worn, camel's-hair mantle!

In his grief, Elisha had torn his own clothes in two pieces; now he took up the mantle of his predecessor. It was as if he tore himself away from his previous role of servant and student, and was ready to assume the authority and power of a prophet of God in his own right. He spent no time in building a shrine to the past, but moved into the future with Elijah's mantle firmly in his grasp. With a sense of determination and destiny, Elisha returned to the Jordan River, and upon its banks he took a deliberate stand. Double-portion power was about to be tested for the first time before an audience of fifty skeptical sons of the prophets.

Without hesitation, he drew the lifeline of decision as he cried out "Where is the Lord God of Elijah?" Words flew into action as Elijah's mantle struck the waters in a mighty move of faith. The word of authority cleaved the waiting water and it rushed to obey, parting this way and that. The newly initiated prophet passed over dry-shod, a rough camel's-hair mantle set straight upon his shoulders. "The spirit of Elijah rests *upon* Elisha!" (II Kings 2:15 TLB). The sons of the prophets never spake truer words. Elisha's subsequent ministry demonstrated the faithfulness of the Lord to honor those who seek to fulfill their calling, not by the might and power of man, but by the Spirit of the living God (Zech. 4:6).

Miracle power characterized the rest of Elisha's life. He was of a totally different personality than Elijah. Elijah was a true child of the desert, rough and ready to speak strong words of judgment backed by fearful demonstrations of God's power— yet tender of heart when touched by human passion. Elisha was a gracious diplomat whose ministry was characterized by miracles of healing and restoration. Undoubtedly the camel's-hair coat was replaced by garb more suited for cities and kings. The true mantle of God's Spirit, however, never left his life, and even in death his dry bones had life-restoring power as one unsuspecting corpse was to discover! (II Kings 13:20–21).

Elisha was an *ordinary* man with a very *ordinary* background, but he was used of God in a very *extraordinary* way. The reason for the contrast lay in the mantle of power which graced his life. To be so clothed with God's Spirit was a precious privilege which was worth more to him than anything else in life. Once the mantle had touched his shoulders there in the meadow setting of his youth, he was spoiled for anything less than the joy which God's purpose and power can bring to human life. To see people healed and restored to their place and ministry in the Kingdom of God brings a happiness which no other earthly pursuit can afford.

MODERN-DAY MANTLES

One almost wistfully reviews the story of Elijah and Elisha, for modern-day mantles of spiritual power and authority are desperately needed, that men might be offered the privilege of freedom which only God's Kingdom can provide. To be governed by God lifts man above the limitations of an unruly world, and releases his life from the lordship of Satan. And it is a possibility, for a greater than Elijah has come—even the Lord Himself.

The mantle of Christ descended from the heavens on the Day of Pentecost, that disciples of ages to come might be clothed with power from on high. As the Father sent His Son to proclaim the Good News of the Kingdom, so the Son sends His believing disciples into the whole world as witnesses of His delivering power. Satan's power can be challenged, and his hold on the hearts of men broken; captives can be released by the authority of God's Word and the power of God's Spirit. The Lord is waiting for His Elishas who will slay their favorite oxen, burn their plows, and follow Him in discipleship. Double-portion power is the privilege for all who are willing to pay the price.

The mantle of power which is to rest upon the lives of Spirit-baptized disciples is not always expressed in a spectacular way. The power of God can be resident within us without any particular sensation to confirm its presence. A king has authority whether he feels like it or not. There is a sense in which we have been made administrators of divine power, for Jesus declared He has given us authority over all the power of the Enemy. The release of God's power and the exercise of divine authority, however, is dependent upon a prior attitude of submission on our part. "Submit (subject) yourselves therefore to God. Resist [withstand] the devil, and he will flee from you" (James 4:7).

The word "submit" in Greek is *hupotasso*. Primarily, this is a military term meaning to "rank under" or "be subordinate to" (*hupo,* under; *tasso,* to arrange). As we come under the authority of God by obediently submitting to and confessing His Word, His Son, and His Spirit, we can triumphantly resist the devil and cause him to flee. As we first "stand with" God, we can then "withstand" the Enemy with divine power and authority. There is, however, one important priority involved. Only as we submit, can we resist.

The theme is reinforced in the next verse: "Draw nigh to God, and he will draw nigh to you" (James 4:8). Again, as we come to God seeking His purpose (will) and His power (way), He will come to us with a wisdom and might that the Enemy cannot withstand. In other words, as we come *under* His authority, His authority comes *upon* us.

DOUBLE-PORTION POWER IN PRACTICE

One morning at a recent conference I felt impressed to leave my hotel room and make my way through the lobby and to the hallways of the nearby convention center. It was as if the Lord had instructed me to make myself available to His leading in regard to someone who might be in spiritual distress. The corridors were practically empty, since no meetings were scheduled at that particular time. Suddenly a door flew open, and a man rushed up to me and exclaimed that he had hoped he might somehow come across my path. He obviously was grievously disturbed, and seemed desperate for help.

He informed me he had just participated in one of the most joyful and powerful meetings in the conference. Everyone had been caught up into a profound spirit of praise, and he had joined with them. Almost immediately after the session concluded, he had been hit like a ton of bricks by dark depression coupled with intense fear. Furthermore, this reaction was a rather common pattern in his life. He shared with me that he had been obsessed since childhood with a fear of going to pieces in public, a scene which always concluded with his death before horrified onlookers.

I told him I could sympathize with him, for when I was a boy, fearful thoughts of death would sometimes overwhelm me. I would become particularly conscious of my heartbeat, which of course would oblige by thumping away, thereby reinforcing the fear. Then we discussed God's promise that He is not the author of fear but of power, love, and a sound mind (II Tim. 1:7). I assured him that I had proven out this promise in my own life.

As we talked further, he indicated that feelings of guilt and fear had plagued him ever since early boyhood. Psychiatric help had brought little relief, and he had practically given up hope of ever being healed. His father had been an alcoholic, and he recalled how he would often return home in a very belligerent mood. His abusive behavior would provoke loud, violent quarrels with his mother, which he could clearly hear in his own room. He never knew just how or when his father would make his appearance in the evening. Often he would hide his head under his pillow, hoping he might avoid the unpleasant encounter. Fear curdled into resentment, and relations with his father were awkward and strained as he entered young manhood. In later years, his father seemed somewhat repentant, and even requested Holy Communion while on his deathbed. Our friend saw his father three hours before his death and hoped there might be a reconciliation with a mutual expression of forgiveness, but communication was impossible. After his death, guilt feelings developed, and he began to question his own salvation. His fear of death was intensified with the thought that he wasn't ready to die.

I shared with him how frequently the Accuser uses this approach, especially with those who have been hurt and scarred by past disappointments and inner distress. My own testimony concerning similar fears built a bridge of hope across which we were going to walk as we approached the healing and releasing power of God's truth. Here was a captive that needed to be set free. Now was the time for the mantle of power to become a ministry of deliverance.

What a joy it was to assure him that it was a rather well-beaten path he was on. But he could expect to meet Jesus there, just as I and many others with similar life stories had done. I could sense faith rising in his heart. No longer was he afraid to face and confess the tragedies and torments of his past. The mantle of God's Spirit covered our lives as we, together with Jesus, confidently withstood Satan to his face. There is a sense of authority that comes when we realize that as we look the devil right square in the eyes, he sees Jesus looking back at him.

Our friend was able to review his childhood with forgiveness in his heart for his father, realizing that in the eternal realm of the Spirit a healing of that personal relationship was still possible. God's forgiveness has the function of washing away the feelings of guilt and fear. Peace came to his heart and covered his face as well. We then confessed the Lordship of Jesus and the healing, releasing power of God's Spirit for him—spirit, soul, and body. We joined hands and put the signature of Jesus to our confession and added the witness of the Holy Spirit as we spontaneously worshiped God together in heavenly tongues of praise. The Lord made it very plain to both of us that it is only His gift of double-portion power which can part the dark waters with which the Enemy would overwhelm our lives. But this is precisely the purpose for which God has placed His Spirit upon our lives.

To be forewarned is to be forearmed. The Lord wisely led us then to discuss the reality of deliverance. It is much more than just a prayer or an experience—essentially it is the Deliverer! Furthermore, He promised never to leave us or forsake us:

He (God) Himself has said, I will not in any way fail you, nor give you up, nor leave you without support. I will not, I will not, I will not in any degree leave you helpless, nor forsake, nor let you down or relax my hold on you—Assuredly not!

So we take comfort and are encouraged, and confidently and boldly say, The Lord is my Helper, I will not be seized with alarm—I will not fear or dread or be terrified! (Heb. 13:5–6 TAB, modified)

The Enemy is a hard loser and will be back around to see how determined we are to stay steady in our confession of faith. In the face of faith, Satan, the roaring lion, becomes a toothless tiger. However, doubt can insert a set of false teeth that can bite pretty hard. We are not to be surprised if the Deceiver roars in our direction a few more times, hoping we will give him back his teeth. Yes, we may still have some of the same tormenting thoughts or feelings flash through our hearts and minds, but now we have the power to recognize their source, submit to the authority of God, and resist the devil. After viewing the tail-end of the tiger disappear over the nearest hill, we will indeed be convinced that a bright, flashy tiger's skin is no match for an old, well-worn camel's-hair mantle.

A Powerful Prescription for Recovery

Sometimes deliverance and inner healing seem to be instantaneous with no further complications. Often, however, there is a time of recovery or convalescence following a crisis time of prayer and release. Some diseases follow a similar pattern. At some point the fever breaks, and healing then progresses to a complete restoration of strength and health. During the time of convalescence, the patient must cooperate with the doctor's orders regarding rest, exercise, diet, and other factors related to his recovery. To ignore the orders hinders the process of healing and can invite a relapse.

Our Great Physician has made every provision for our

complete recovery, and has promised even greater strength and vitality than we have ever experienced in the past. We must submit to His prescription for health, however, if we are to effectively resist the deteriorating powers of disease. The following is a divine prescription for the convalescent:

1. VITAMIN PILLS OF PRAISE

   God lives in the praises of his people (Ps. 22:3). Something of His life is imparted to us during times of praise, whether we feel like it or not. An attitude of thanksgiving has both a positive and prolonged effect upon our well-being. Like vitamins, praise acts as a catalyst and enhances and harmonizes all of our spiritual life processes. The little phrase, "Praise the Lord," is a powerful pill which should be taken throughout the day.

2. MERRY-HEART MEDICINE

   "A [merry] happy heart is a good medicine and a cheerful mind works healing, but a broken spirit dries the bones!" (Prov. 17:22 TAB). Weak, anemic Christians are joyless Christians; and joyless Christians become weak, anemic Christians. Basically, joy is not a feeling but a person— JESUS! Therefore we have joy whether we feel joyful or not. That confession can elicit the corresponding emotion. God has given us power to overcome melancholy moods, and we need to deliberately draw upon it. "The joy of the Lord is your strength!" (Neh. 8:10).

3. THE HEALING OIL OF FORGIVENESS

   Is anyone among you sick? He should call in the church elders . . . and they should pray over him, anointing him with oil in the Lord's name. And the prayer of faith will *save* him that is sick, and the Lord will *restore* him; and if he has committed sins, he will be *forgiven*. Confess to one another your faults; and pray for one another that you may be *healed* and *restored*—to a spiritual tone of mind and heart. (James 5:14–16 TAB, italics mine)

   We need to maintain a clear relationship with one another and the Lord. It is good to keep short accounts with God, for the oil of His forgiveness has antiseptic properties which can defend us against reinfection.

4. THE TONIC OF SPIRITUAL FELLOWSHIP

Let us hold fast the confession of our hope without wavering, for He who promised is faithful; and let us consider how to *stimulate* one another to love and good deeds, not forsaking our assembling together, as is the habit of some, but *encouraging* one another; and all the more, as you see the day drawing near. (Heb. 10:23–25 NASB, italics mine)

We need the *stimulation* and *encouragement* which can only be found in the fellowship of the faithful. Fellowship is a powerful antidote for the failing heart. We have not been created to go it alone. We all need each other very much— God planned it so.

5. A BALANCED DIET FROM GOD'S WORD

The fresh bread of God's Word is a daily necessity. "Man shall not live by bread alone, but by every word that proceedeth out of the mouth of God" (Matt. 4:4). Jesus is the word made flesh, and through the written word He becomes for us the Bread of Life. Our privilege and responsibility is to rely upon the Holy Spirit to relate our need to God's answer in Christ Jesus as promised in His Word. God's Spirit can sort out the particular promise which we are to personally claim in faith. The Holy Scriptures are to become the staff and strength of our daily life. God has a word for you today. Have you received it?

6. THE FRESH AIR OF PRAYER

"I will pray with the spirit, and I will pray with the understanding also" (I Cor. 14:15). Prayer should be as natural as breathing, for in one sense it becomes for us the very breath of life. The vitality of prayer is not based primarily in the one who prays, but in Him to whom we pray. An attitude of faith and submission will lift our prayers beyond our feelings that God's Word and will can be performed through our lives on earth—as that word and will has already been fulfilled in heaven. There is a Man in the heavens who is touched by the feelings of our earthly infirmities. He is most willing to bare His mighty arm on our behalf.

7. THE PURE WATERS OF GOD'S SPIRIT

Refreshing rivers of life-giving water are promised to those believers who truly thirst after God in their time of need and desire (John 7:37–38). The fruit and gifts of the Spirit become to us streams of life during our desert experiences. These are expressions of God's grace which can overflow in the daily life of every Spirit-filled child of God. This should be our holy expectation.

8. THE REST OF PEACE

"Come unto me . . . and I will give you rest" (Matt. 11:28). Jesus is our peace, and in Him all conflict ceases. Such rest is absolutely essential if we are to face the demands of each day spiritually refreshed. For this reason we are cautioned to guard this peace with care, and allow it to be the basis for settling all decisions as they arise (Col. 3:15). We can willfully open the door of our minds (and imaginations) to the godless side of our circumstances and lose the peace only His presence can bring (Isa. 26:3). It is amazing that although in prison, Paul always had enough grace and peace that he could share it with others in the introduction of his epistles. "Grace and peace be yours from God our Father and the Lord Jesus Christ."

9. A REHABILITATION PROGRAM

To rehabilitate means to re-outfit (re-equip) for work. This means turning our attention from ourselves to others and their needs and allowing God to work through us on their behalf. We don't have to wait for full recovery to share what we have, where we are, with whomever the Lord brings our way. We might even want to go out of our way and actually seek somebody to whom we can minister. Our own healing is enhanced as we share God's healing power with others. "Whatever good any one does, he will receive the same again from the Lord" (Eph. 6:8 RSV).

10. THE EXERCISE OF FAITH

God never requires us to exercise more faith than we have; but the measure that's been given, He does expect (Rom. 12:3). The Lord requires that we obediently and faithfully follow His orders. There is a part we play in obtaining and maintaining our inner healing. The Lord knows what size steps we are able to take in faith, and He will clearly set the path before us. All of us are ready for the next step, but only we can make that move. It requires an exercise of our will in faith to open the floodgates of spiritual power. It is "as we go" that God confirms His Word with signs following (Mark 16:20).

THE LORDSHIP OF JESUS CHRIST

God has put the *mantle* of His Spirit upon our shoulders, the *scepter* of authority in our hand, and the *word* of faith in our mouths, that we might assume the privileges and responsibilities of sonship. So often we lose by default because we do not decisively confess the Lordship of our Christ who rules and reigns on earth wherever and whenever that confession is made.

After I had ministered this truth one morning in a summer camp, a woman came forward requesting that she might be released from a bondage of fear. She came in faith, and there was a certain sense of defined deliberation in the manner with which she knelt for prayer before the onlooking congregation. The mantle of God's authority rested upon that moment, and as we confessed the yoke-breaking power of the Holy Spirit, I saw in my spirit an image of Satan as a dark, shadowy form, reluctantly giving way as we prayed. I described the scene with great feeling to the congregation, for the Enemy was slowly bending his knee, and bowing his head, and was forced to confess with us the Lordship of Jesus Christ.

The atmosphere was electric with the power of God's presence, and dramatic things began to happen throughout the entire assembly. One woman cried out with a loud voice, and actually fell from her chair as the Lord released her from Satan's power and flooded her life with joy and peace. An elderly woman came running down the aisle shouting, "I am healed, I am healed!" I had seen her the night before, because she had hobbled to the front on her cane requesting prayer for cancer. It was a different woman altogether who joyfully confessed the liberating power of Jesus which had set her free spiritually and physically. I have since learned that her healing was permanent, and she continues to praise the Lord for His goodness.

Throughout the day, others shared with me what the releasing power of God's Spirit had accomplished in their lives. Some of their testimonies have been shared in previous chapters. Why did it happen? We had confessed that Jesus is Lord. His Lordship confers upon us an authority over all of the power of the Enemy that would oppose the will of God in our lives.

CONCLUDING CHALLENGE

Once more we are reminded that the Lord will either *protect* us from, *deliver* us out of, or *perfect* us through any situation we may face, if we confess the Lordship of Jesus. The work of His Spirit may be instantaneous or progressive; He will either change our circumstances, or change us in our circumstances; but there can always be an inner, spiritual healing, regardless. Many times the Lord requires us to cooperate in faith with *His* method of healing, for not only is this a means toward our own maturity, but it becomes a bridge into other peoples' lives. Our storm may persist, but once we have found our footing, we can stabilize those who are around us, because we are within touching distance and have a fellow-feeling for their infirmities. Like the apostle Paul, we, too, regardless of circumstances, can be filled in such measure with God's grace and peace that there is enough to share with others who look to us for help.

We face a variety of painful events in our daily lives. There will be times of sadness and loneliness when others don't understand, but God will provide. Should these be your circumstances this very hour, His provision has already been made: for there at your feet will be found an old, well-worn camel's-hair mantle. "Arise, the Jordan River is not far hence!"

9

HIS SPIRIT OUTPOURED
Anointed and Appointed

Moreover the Lord said to Moses, Take the finest spices: flowing myrrh . . . sweet-smelling cinnamon . . . fragrant calamus . . . cassia . . . and olive oil. Compound all of this according to the art of the perfumer into a holy *anointing* oil . . . and you shall *anoint* Aaron and his sons, and sanctify (consecrate, separate) them that they may minister to me as priests. And say to the sons of Israel, this is a holy *anointing* oil (symbol of the Holy Spirit) sacred to me alone. . . . It must never be *poured* upon an ordinary person (layman's body—literally, the flesh of man). . . . It is holy, and you shall hold it sacred. (Exod. 30:22–25, 30–32 various versions)

Behold, how good and how pleasant it is for brethren to dwell together in unity! It is like the precious ointment *poured* on the head, that ran down on the beard, even the beard of Aaron the first high priest, that came down upon the collar and skirts of his garments consecrating the whole body. (ps. 133:1–2 TAB, modified)

So too Christ, the Messiah, did not exalt Himself to be made a high priest, but was *appointed* and exalted by Him Who said to Him, You are My Son, today I have begotten You; As He says also in another place, You are a Priest *appointed* forever after the order (rank) of Melchizedek. (Heb. 5:5–6 TAB, modified)

God *anointed* Jesus of Nazareth with the Holy Ghost and with power. (Acts 10:38)

The Spirit of the Lord God is upon me; because the Lord hath *anointed* me. (Isa. 61:1)

Inasmuch then as we have a great High Priest Who has . . . ascended and passed through the heavens, Jesus the Son of God, let us hold fast our confession [of faith in Him]. (Heb. 4:14 TAB)

This Jesus God raised up, and of that all we His disciples are witnesses. Being therefore lifted high by the right hand of God, and having received from the Father the promised Holy Spirit, He has made this *outpouring* which you yourselves both see and hear. (Acts 2:32–33 TAB, modified)

And it shall come to pass in the last days, God declares, that I will *pour* out of My Spirit upon all mankind. . . . Yes, and on My menservants also and on My maidservants in those days I will *pour* out of My Spirit, and they shall prophesy. (Acts 2:17–18 TAB, italics mine)

And all the Jewish believers who had come with Peter were amazed because the Gift of the Holy Spirit had actually been *poured* out upon the Gentiles. (Acts 10:45 various versions)

It is God Who confirms and establishes us in joint fellowship with you in Christ [The Anointed One], and has consecrated and *anointed* us—enduing us with the gifts of the Holy Spirit. (II Cor. 1:21 TAB, modified)

But—you hold a sacred *appointment,* you have been given an unction—you have been *anointed* by the Holy One, and you all know the Truth. The *anointing* (sacred appointment, unction) which you received from Him, abides permanently in you. (I John 2:20,27 TAB, modified)

ANOINTING: ITS MEANING AND SIGNIFICANCE

The word "anointing" in Hebrew is *mashach*. It refers to the pouring of sacred oil upon people, places, or things which have been set apart for divine recognition. The first use of the term *mashach* relates to Jacob pouring oil upon his stone pillow, following his ladder-to-heaven dream. After dedicating the place by this ceremonial procedure, he dignified it with the name Bethel (house of God).

The next time the term is used is in connection with the consecration and sanctification of Aaron as the first high priest. Psalm 133 describes how Aaron was dramatically dressed in all of his official vestments. Moses lifted the vessel of sacred oil freshly compounded for the occasion, and Aaron sensed the warm, sweet anointing as it softly saturated the hair of his head. Moses kept on pouring. The fragrant oil flowed down upon Aaron's face and neck, and soon his beard glistened with the anointing in the bright desert sun. Moses poured profusely until every fiber in the fabric of Aaron's priestly garment, from the seamless collar to the skirts below, was permeated with the perfumed oil. When the ordination service was finally finished, everyone knew Aaron had been anointed.

Not only priests, but prophets and kings were initiated into their ministry by ceremonial anointing. Even material things were anointed with holy oil to consecrate them for sacred service. The tabernacle, its parts and appointments, were all dedicated with sacred oil. In each case, there were the companion concepts of dedication and designation, a separation for some specific, sacred purpose. In other words, there was an *appointment* with the *anointing*.

In the ordination of individuals, the anointing was not only an emblematic ritual; it actually imparted the spiritual qualities necessary to equip them for their office. God's purpose and power would be their abiding provision if they continued to walk before the Lord in faith and obedience. The Old Testament is filled with examples of prophets, priests, and kings who faithfully ministered under their anointing. King David is a beautiful illustration:

And the Lord said to Samuel . . . "Fill your horn with oil, and go; I will send you to Jesse the Bethlehemite, for I have selected a king for Myself among his sons. . . . Now [David] was ruddy, with beautiful eyes and a handsome appearance. And the Lord said, "Arise, anoint him; for this is he." Then Samuel took the horn of oil and anointed him in the midst of his brothers; and the Spirit of the Lord came mightily upon David from that day forward. (I Sam. 16:1, 12–13 NASB)

The Hebrew word *mashach* is the root from which the name *Messiah* is derived. *Messiah* means "anointed"! In the Greek language, the word for anointing is *chrisma*. "The Messiah" in Greek is *ho Christos*, obviously derived from the same term and transliterated into English as "the Christ" (the Anointed). The spiritual significance of the sacred rituals, forms, and offices of Jewish life were fulfilled in Jesus Christ. In the Old Testament, individuals set apart for the office of prophet, priest, or king were often called, "the Lord's Anointed." They were lively types of One who was to come, namely, the Christ. As a prophet, He would speak to us of God's love and truth; as our High Priest, He would offer the supreme sacrifice for our sins; and as the King of kings, He would establish the Kingdom of God in our hearts and in our homes.

The anointing of Aaron, the first high priest, is a beautiful picture of the Lord Jesus Christ our Great High Priest. He too was abundantly anointed—*without measure* (John 3:34 NASB). Upon His ascension to the right hand of the Father for His priestly intercession on our behalf, Christ, the exalted Head of His Church, received the promised oil of God's Holy Spirit and *poured* it forth upon the many members which make up His Body on earth below. In one sense, Holy Spirit Baptism is a mighty anointing from the Father, through the Son, for our initiation into a life of dedicated service. We, too, have a royal priestly and prophetic ministry to fulfill as sons and daughters of the King.

AN ABIDING ANOINTING

As we *abide* in the Anointed One, and He *abides* in us, there is established an *abiding* relationship with His anointing. The apostle John makes this very clear in his first epistle:

> The *anointing* which you received from Him *abides* permanently in you, and you have no need that anyone teach you. Just as His *anointing* truthfully teaches you all things, you must as taught, *abide* (permanently live, deeply rooted and knitted) in Him. (I John 2:27 various versions)

To abide in Christ is to abide in His anointing. The word "abide" (*meno*) refers to a permanent, living relationship, involving unbroken fellowship. As we steadfastly submit to the Lordship of Jesus in faith, love, and obedience, we will be continually covered by His anointing. Recognition of His Lordship is an essential prerequisite for the full flow of His Spirit. It is the fountainhead from which the streams of the Spirit spring forth:

> The LORD said unto my Lord, Sit thou at my right hand. . . . Therefore being at the right hand of God exalted and having received of the Father the promise of the Holy Spirit, He has poured forth this which you now see and hear. (Acts 2:34,33 various versions)

The abiding quality of Christ's anointing for the obedient disciple is a powerful concept which the Enemy does not want us to recognize. He has partially succeeded in obscuring the truth by distorting the definition of anointing in our minds. For many, the term is equated with a specific feeling, or restricted to particular manifestations of the Spirit. If both are absent, one concludes the anointing is, too. We fail to realize that the anointing is not something we pray or feel for, but something that we confess.

Many times I have prayed that God would anoint the meeting, music, speaker, and listeners with His Spirit. This is a perfectly good prayer to the extent it confesses our dependency upon the Holy Spirit. The Deceiver, however, would love to cast doubt into our hearts with the fear that maybe God won't anoint us. We look to our feelings for confirmation of the Spirit's anointing, and if we are feeling low, may decide that the occasion is going to be another one of those dry runs. We need to recognize that the anointing abides whether we feel like it or not. Our responsibility is to make this our confession, and faithfully submit ourselves to the direction which the ever-flowing Spirit is ready to reveal.

It is true the presence of the Holy Spirit may evoke certain emotional or even physical responses. Some recognize a familiar feeling of joy, power, or weeping. Others feel a warm, tingling sensation, or perhaps experience little chills or goose bumps; but certainly the anointing from our Lord cannot be limited to something as unstable as physical or emotional responses.

THE ANOINTING: CONFESSED AND EXPRESSED

There have been times when I have been greatly moved within by the stirring of God's Spirit. On other occasions, I have felt very little except perhaps tired and somewhat depressed. Yet in God's grace, when a need would arise and I would move in faith—because it was the right direction to take in obedience—the Holy Spirit has provided wisdom and power far beyond my limitations. I was in a meeting on one occasion that was so lifeless and restrained I honestly wished I hadn't come. I had planned to speak on Kingdom-power but in light of the dismal circumstances, I began toying with the idea of giving a little devotional thought from the Psalms and leaving the whole scene as soon as possible.

The Lord then reminded me that I had prayed during the week to become a man of faith as Jesus was. I was impressed that many of the synagogue situations He faced were probably pretty dead when He arrived, but by the time He was through ministering under the anointing, life had sprung forth. I took the initiative, claimed the anointing, and preached on King-dom-power. I then boldly invited those who wanted prayer to come forward for personal ministry. The pastor promptly arose, gave the benediction, and dismissed the congregation, without providing an opportunity for any prayer-ministry whatsoever. The people all streamed for the doors, while I slipped back into my depression, wondering what I was supposed to do next. I decided I would play it to the hilt in faith, even if it meant standing alone at the front until the last person left.

I wasn't alone for long, however, for a little white-haired woman came forward and requested prayer for pain which she feared was related to the recurrence of a former cancer condition. How reassuring it would have been to have sensed the healing power of God pulsating through an arm prickly with goose bumps; but I didn't feel anything—except totally inadequate. I did, however, confess the anointing which abides and made a move in faith, which turned out to be a word of wisdom. I suggested we worship the Lord together before praying and claim His faithfulness. As we began to bless God in spiritual tongues of praise, He began to move in a manifest way. The power of the Lord came upon her with such a physical force, I had to support her to keep her from falling. As we then confessed God's healing power, her pain left, and the situation became a most joyful occasion. Others came forward as well, and God's blessing was evident in a most gracious way.

It was a lesson for me concerning the anointing that abides. I had confessed the faithfulness of the Holy Spirit in spite of my feelings. God's Word had been proclaimed, and He honored it. The Spirit of Wisdom had set a direction which, when followed in faith and obedience, led to the fulfillment of His will for those involved. The same story has been repeated many times in principle, covering a variety of circumstances. What confidence and hope this abiding ministry of the Holy Spirit can bring to our lives during times of confusion and discouragement! As we move in God's will, His Spirit will perform His Word as it is proclaimed to His people.

FRESH OIL ALWAYS AVAILABLE

Once we begin to appreciate the abiding work of the Holy Spirit, the Enemy would seek to move us to another extreme— that of presumption. If His anointing always abides, we might be tempted to take God's presence for granted, rather than realizing our responsibility to be sensitive and submissive to the Spirit's leading. The anointing does indeed abide, but the manifestation of the Holy Spirit in harmony with God's will depends upon our humbling ourselves before the Lord in faith and obedience. The gentle dove of God's Spirit is easily grieved, and our insensitivity can limit His freedom of expression in our midst.

There is a balance between our recognition of God's abiding presence and the special visitations of the Holy Spirit which arise from that presence. I once asked the Lord for an example from Scripture that would illustrate this truth. I was reminded of Elijah's encounter with the widow of Zarephath (I Kings 17). As he had prophesied, a great drought afflicted the land. Elijah had been fed by ravens by the brook Cherith until it, too, had dried up. God then instructed him to go to Zarephath where He had planned for Elijah to dwell in the home of a widow who would provide for him and her son.

At this point the widow was totally unaware of the divine role she was to play. Elijah encountered her picking up sticks at the city gate, and he requested that she bring him some water and a morsel of bread. Although a Gentile, she implied some recognition of Jehovah in her response: "As the Lord your God lives . . . I have . . . only a handful of meal . . . and a little oil . . . which I intended to bake for me and my son that we may eat it, and die!" (I Kings 17:12 TAB, modified). Elijah assured her through a prophetic word that the meal would not waste away nor the oil fail until the Lord sent rain upon the earth. He then requested she make his cake *first* and afterward bake for herself and her son. She could neither see nor feel the *anointing* that rested upon Elijah; all she had was the prophetic *word* which she obeyed. She soon discovered the provision resident in the anointing. It was beautifully symbolized by the never-failing vessel of oil. There was always a sufficient supply of oil for a fresh outpouring as the specific need arose. Apparently a little oil always remained in the vessel (the anointing which abides), which was the ever-present source of each new outpouring (special visitations). Each time, faith brought the oil and meal together to meet their daily need for the bread of life.

Many ingredients were compounded in the preparation of the sacred oil. They were precisely measured and blended according to specified proportions. Likewise there are a diversity of ministries when it comes to the fragrant expressions of God's Holy Spirit. How careful we must be not to limit our concept of the anointing by relating it to specific times, places, personalities, or manifestations. There is a distinctive anointing for all occasions, and it is our responsibility to recognize the sovereignty of God's Spirit and submit to His gracious desires. This is not a passive permissiveness, but a sensitive searching out of God's will and purpose. It also involves a unity of heart and mind which will command the Lord's blessing and allow the oil of the Spirit to freely and freshly flow over the entire fellowship as so vividly portrayed in Psalm 133.

Many times I have been prompted to wait upon the Lord and allow God's people time to clear their spirits and join together in sensitive expectation. It is so easy for us to rush presumptuously into our programmed meeting. We may have a meeting, but it won't be with the Lord, for this is totally dependent upon the ministry of the Holy Spirit. We can meet with people, words, and rituals and still miss God altogether. All the while, the precious anointing waits to be recognized and appreciated.

"Lord, forgive us for being such clods on occasions when You were so ready to go far beyond our expectations. May the fresh oil of Your Spirit wash our souls and make our spirits clear and bright with holy anticipation, we earnestly pray."

APPOINTED AND ANOINTED

We are not only divinely anointed, but also divinely appointed. Following Holy Spirit Baptism, individuals intuitively sense a divinely appointed purpose for their lives. They are eager to know what the Lord's will is concerning their place and function in the Body of Christ. There is an awareness of divine destiny, and they are drawn to the Lord for His guidance and direction that it might be fulfilled. We are indeed anointed for ministry and will feel restless until our mission in life is achieved. Scripture declares man has been born with this inner sense of eternal purpose:

He also has planted eternity in men's heart and mind [a divinely implanted sense of a purpose working through the ages which nothing under the sun, but only God, can satisfy]. (Eccles. 3:11 TAB)

Men of destiny are men of dignity. Noble purpose confers a nobility upon those who are called to fulfill that purpose. There is a need for nobility and a desire for dignity which has been born in the soul of every individual—God planned it so. Self-respect is rooted in our sense of mission for life. Only worthy goals can bring an awareness of worthwhileness to our existence. Defined purpose has a definite integrating effect upon our personality. Everything works together for good to those who have a divine mission or purpose in life (Rom. 8:28). To be filled with the Holy Spirit is to be filled with a divine sense of destiny.

Satan, of course, does not want our lives to be related to divine purpose (God's will). He will either divert us into a lazy, aimless existence or drive us into pursuits which are devoid of eternal significance. There is a temporary satisfaction to be found in both, depending upon our personality makeup. Once we become alive to the Holy Spirit and are acutely aware that we do have a divine destiny, Satan switches to another tactic—to instill in us a fear of missing God's will and the ministry to which we have been called. Satan achieves this by perverting and distorting our concept and definition of ministry. We will respond to his deception by either fruitlessly wandering around in great frustration trying to discover God's will, or presumptuously leaping into action without proper preparation or direction. It occurs to me as I write, that I have done some of both on different occasions. Maybe the thought occurred to you as well. I suppose to the Lord it looks like some of us are hopping about like nervous fleas, while others of us are wandering around like ants who have lost their nest. If we once get airborne, we can learn how to make efficient beelines between the honey-hive and the fragrant flowers.

God does want us to find our place and function in His family, for in no other way can we redeem the time and fill our lives with His purpose. He has sent to us the Comforter as the Spirit of truth to teach and train us, that we might rightfully possess a knowledge of His will:

> Look carefully then how you walk! Live purposefully *and* worthily *and* accurately, not as the unwise and witless, but as wise—sensible, intelligent people; Making the very most of the time . . . because the days are evil. Therefore do not be vague *and* thoughtless *and* foolish, but understanding and firmly grasping what the will of the Lord is. And do not get drunk with wine . . . but ever be filled . . . with the (Holy) Spirit. (Eph. 5:15–18 TAB)

Surely we are being encouraged in this passage not to become intoxicated with the spirit of doubt, fear, or frustration. Nor are we to be stimulated by the wine of hasty presumption. But we are to be filled with the Holy Spirit, who can graciously provide us with wisdom, knowledge, and discernment concerning the will of God.

What Is My Ministry?

Very often when ministries are mentioned, we think of the fivefold offices outlined by Paul in his Ephesian letter: "And He (Christ) appointed to the church apostles, prophets, evangelists, pastors and teachers" (Eph. 4:11 various versions). Most of the people related to the community life of the New Testament church probably didn't officially fall into any of the above categories. Certainly no novices were so recognized, and individuals never established their own calling. This is not to say that some of the functions of the above offices were not expressed in a more general way. Surely there were many who were actively sharing their faith, caring for new converts, prophesying, etc., but not in the unique sense of an official ministry. A divine office involved a divine appointment which would be recognized and confirmed by the spiritual leaders in the community. Such ministries would indeed arise out of a fellowship of life in Christ, but there would be many other callings as well.

As a developing child needs the counsel and protection of an earthly family, so God's servants need to mature within the safety that community life can provide. Both men and their ministries need to be proven on home ground before being exposed in a more extensive way. The call of God may eventually lead some to strange and faraway places; others will spend a lifetime in one setting; both can know the satisfaction of God's perfect will, and find their lives fulfilled in performing His divine purpose. It all begins by taking our place in a local fellowship and expecting God to disclose our function as He has ordained it.

All ministry should be grounded in love, and this provides a pattern for priority. We are exhorted to love God, and others as ourselves. The order seems to be: God, self, then others. This would mean our ministry should first be to the Lord, then to ourselves, followed by our ministry to others (Matt. 22:37–39).

Ministry to God

Our ministry to God involves our praise, and since we are to live to the praise of His glory, this will involve every area of our life. All that we do is to be a loving ministry to the Lord.

In every work that [Hezekiah] began in the service of the house of God, and in the law, and in the commandments, to seek his God, he did it with all his heart, and prospered. (II Chron. 31:21)

For whether we live, we live unto the Lord! (Rom. 14:8)

Whatever may be your task, work at it heartily as something done for the Lord and not for men, knowing with all certainty that it is from the Lord, and not men. Then you will receive your inheritance which is your real reward. The One whom you are actually serving is the Lord Christ. (Col. 3:23–24 TAB, modified)

This truth is to become operational where we are. If what we are doing is not acceptable to the Lord, our ministry to Him involves an immediate change. If it is a task which is acceptable, we should henceforth recognize the Lord as our unseen superior. God may lead us on to other responsibilities, but until He does, we minister to Him in our present situation. What a different perspective this brings to our concept of spiritual service.

Obviously, our ministry to the Lord includes our worship and adoration of Himself for Himself. Those in places of great physical limitation can minister to the Lord in praise and realize their lonely hours are by no means wasted. We can praise God in all things for the good which He will bring forth on behalf of those who love Him and recognize their call to the most precious ministry of worship. Unusually great will be their heavenly reward.

I once prayed with a middle-aged woman whom I hadn't seen since her early teens. The beauty of youth had long since been destroyed by the devastating powers of chronic disease. I was shocked to see her withered form, and saddened by her loss of speech. She could understand what was said, however, and I sought for some words of encouragement for one of God's handmaidens whose life seemed such a total loss in terms of earthly standards.

The Lord prompted me to encourage her in her ministry of worship to Him. Like Mary of old, her portion was the perfume of praise as she anointed His feet with her tears. We joined hands and worshiped together, the Holy Spirit of prayer lifting us beyond earthly bondages into the very heart of God. We were on holy ground, and heaven seemed very near. Worship can sanctify any situation. She has since been called to her heavenly home, and I know her ministry of love to her Lord has already won for her a special place in His presence.

MINISTRY TO OURSELVES

There is a sense in which we can and should minister God's love to ourselves. The Psalmist suggests we can commune with our heart upon our bed (Ps. 4:4;77:6). He speaks to his soul (inner self) as if it were a close friend. "Why art thou cast down, O my soul? . . . Hope thou in God!" (Ps. 42:5). Sometimes he exhorts his soul to worship: "Bless the Lord, O my soul, and all that is within me, bless his holy name. Bless the Lord, O my soul, and forget not all his benefits!" (Ps. 103:1–2). Are you on friendly terms with your soul, or is there some inner hostility? Are you at war or peace with yourself? Do you love and appreciate your soul, or do you despise yourself?

God gave us our souls (selves) to be loved, appreciated, and developed for His glory and our good. Jesus declares it is a great loss if a man loses his own soul. Our selfhood is precious in God's sight, for it possesses the potential for great glory when it is surrendered to the control and ministry of His Spirit. When we are filled with the Holy Spirit, we have the privilege and responsibility of ministering the life of Jesus to our own souls. As we become strong in the inner man, we can then minister to others. In fact, to the extent we hate or depreciate ourselves, it will be impossible to really love or appreciate others in any effective way.

God's grace can re-order our divine love-life. First, He expresses His love to us while we are yet sinners (Rom. 5:8). As we truly accept that love, we can love ourselves, for His love confers a lovely quality to our lives which is to progressively develop. Now we can love others and minister God's life to them as it was expressed to us in Christ Jesus. Love has a divine way of reproducing itself. In this context, we can see that self-ministry is an essential link in the chain of God's love, for only through us can it ultimately reach others.

What is it that we are to minister to ourselves, that we in turn might become effective in our outreach to others? We might view this theme by considering our responsibilities to our physical self, or outer man (body), and our non-physical self, or inner man (spirit-soul complex).

Outer-Man Ministry

The inner man is housed in and dependent upon the functions of the body for its vitality in the earthly, temporal sense. If our bodies are weary, our minds become dull and finally fade into the unconsciousness of sleep. An active spiritual communion may continue while we sleep, since God neither slumbers nor sleeps (Ps. 121:3–4) and our spirit is one (joined) with His Spirit (I Cor. 6:17). This activity, however, will not be registered or appreciated at the mental level—except occasionally through dreams. In other words, we may be spiritually alive and alert while mentally tired and physically weary, but our physical bodies limit the expression of that life as far as earthly ministry is concerned. Even Jesus Christ found it necessary to come aside for physical rest and refreshment and encouraged His disciples to do likewise (Mark 6:31–32).

We need to minister to our bodies, recognizing they are the temples of the Holy Spirit (I Cor. 6:19). His ministry through our physical bodies to an earthly world will be restricted if we are careless and undisciplined about our rest, diet, exercise, and recreation. There have been times I have had to repent for overeating, and becoming dull physically and spiritually because of indifferent indulgence. Other times I have been so "busy for the Lord," I have missed meals, lost sleep, and expended myself beyond the Lord's will. Ultimately, I have paid for my negligence, with more lost time in recuperation than I had gained in burning myself out for God. On some occasions, I have had the distinct impression that I had remained behind for further fellowship long after the Lord had gone to bed: the next day He was ready for a far more vigorous pace than the short night's rest had prepared me for.

Physical well-being is never an end in itself, as some food faddists and physical culturists have made it out to be. But when it is learned that excess weight, for instance, can reduce our life expectancy by six to ten years, one finds a direct correlation between physical fitness and opportunity for ongoing ministry for the Lord. God never holds us responsible for physical limitations beyond our control (and will even redeem such handicaps), but He does require that we respect and care for our bodies, that we may be faithful ministers of His Spirit. It is His desire that we diligently discipline ourselves physically that we might be at our best spiritually. Discipleship involves the body as well as the spirit and soul. As we are careful concerning our part in body ministry, we can expect God to lift us far beyond our physical weaknesses in special times of unusual demand.

Many times I have blamed my body for not holding up under some of the sustained pressures to which I have subjected it. I can't even remember when I have praised it in the Lord, for performing well and thereby allowing me to share God's love with others. Our earthly temples come in a variety of sizes, shapes, and degrees of beauty, but all of them deserve our respect and appreciation, because they enable us to express *without,* the glory of God we have experienced *within.*

I have never seen a truly Spirit-filled person whose inner beauty didn't shine through their physical being regardless of its imperfections. What a wonderful day it will be when we receive our glorified bodies, and can perfectly respond to and express the light and love of God without any limitation whatsoever (I Cor. 15:42–44). In the meantime, may we appreciate our earthly temples as a gracious promise of that which is to come.

Inner-Man Ministry

Our inner man is the spirit-soul complex which has been quickened by the saving grace of God's Spirit. Unlike our physical bodies, which disintegrate while awaiting their final glorified form, the renewed inner man possesses an eternal integrity. "To be absent from the body [is] to be present with the Lord" (II Cor. 5:8). The Lord of glory is also the believer's judge who will evaluate his earthly (soulish) life. Thoughts, words, and deeds will be tried as by fire with eternal reward in view (I Cor. 3:11–15; II Cor. 5:1–10).

Many of the Lord's parables indicate we are to be laying up eternal treasure in heaven (Matt. 6:19–20). It is at the level of our spirit-soul life that we become conformed into His image. It is that picture which determines our reward in heaven. Rewards will, without doubt, be related to our capacity to enjoy and express the life of Christ throughout the ages. A friend of mine had a vision of heaven. Among other things, he saw people as glasses, all filled to over-flowing, but of different capacities.

As we cultivate (minister to) the life of our inner man, we will become more like Jesus in character and conduct. What are some of our selfhood ministries which will enable us to become spiritually strong and healthy within? (Again, this is a prerequisite to a strong healthy ministry *without*.) Some specific functions follow:

1. FORGIVENESS

   Having received God's forgiveness, and forgiven others in His love, we must also minister forgiveness to ourselves. No one else (even God) can fulfill this function. What the Lord has cleansed, we are not to call unclean. The anointing of God's Holy Spirit can break the yoke of an unforgiving spirit with regard not only to others—but also to ourselves. It might well be in order to ask *ourselves* to forgive *ourselves* for holding an unforgiving attitude toward *ourselves*. I recall repeatedly blaming myself over and over again for something, when the Spirit interrupted my broken-record rehearsal by asking me if I thought my little fault was greater than the forgiveness Jesus gave His life for on the Cross. I was informed that when Christ cried out, "It is finished!" it was; and I might just as well finish-out my self-condemnation as well. I did.

2. DELIVERANCE

   A woman almost on the point of hysteria called our home and pleaded with me to pray for her because she was under terrible bondage and depression. I refused. Knowing how God was working in her life, I suggested she rise up in faith, confess her anointing and authority as a daughter of the King, rebuke the Enemy, and decisively complete the task the Lord had assigned for her to do. She was to deliver herself. I would agree with her in prayer. She prayed and released herself from her self-induced state of distress. Sometimes when we open the door and invite the devil in, God expects us to drive him out, shut the door, and get back to business again.

   On another occasion, a couple asked me to pray for them because the wife was plagued by fearful and tormenting imaginations and unpleasant dreams. After sharing together for a time, it became apparent to me that she had no concept of the power and authority which was for her own deliverance. She was pitifully (and faithlessly) praying that God would somehow help her. I assured her that she was to submit to God and then directly and decisively rebuke Satan, realizing that the releasing word of faith was nigh—even upon her lips. Her responsibility was to speak it, and stand her ground as an appointed handmaiden of God. We sealed our time of counsel with prayer and confessed the Lordship of Jesus. Tears turned into joy, the cloud lifted, and once more the truth concerning *self-deliverance* through the anointing that abides had set someone free.

3. HEALING

It is possible to administer many of the principles of healing which have been discussed earlier to the hurts in our own lives once we recognize that truth. Some of our previous illustrations are examples of personal healing-of-self ministries. The woman whose tearful mother was an alcoholic actually was shown her own emotional problem by the Lord. She claimed her inner healing in the name of Jesus and progressively recovered. Now she is an anointed Bible teacher. I know another woman who won her victory over a cancer condition by memorizing verses on divine healing from the Scriptures and steadfastly confessing them to herself and the Lord. My own progressive healing from an inferiority complex was claimed by applying the healing word and truth of God to painful parts of my own life. Nobody can minister healing to others with compassion and understanding like those who have personally claimed and experienced it in their own lives.

4. COUNSEL

Many times we need to counsel ourselves from Scripture and with the words of wisdom which the Holy Spirit gives in our times of need. If we don't minister spiritual encouragement to ourselves, the devil won't! We probably spend more time talking and listening to ourselves than we do to any other person. Maybe we should be more careful what we say. Furthermore, what we speak in the *silence* of our hearts, can be so *loud* to our inner ears that we hear very little else. What we *say* on the inside will determine what we *are* on the outside. "As a man thinketh (inner voice) in his heart so *is* he" (Prov. 23:7). Many times I have talked myself into discouragement and despair. There have also been times when I have rather sternly disciplined myself, and given heed to my own ministry of counsel in the Lord. If we can't rule our own spirit, how can we effectively counsel others? "Soul, why art thou cast down within me? Hope thou in God!"

5. PROTECTION

Sometimes we need to protect the inner man from unnecessary abuse. There are enough bruises in our natural course of life and ministry without exposing ourselves needlessly to stressing situations with which God never intended for us to be involved. The Deceiver is pleased to draw us into all kinds of enervating skirmishes which are quite apart from the divine directives which the Lord has set for our path.

King David inquired of the Lord on two separate occasions concerning battle with the Philistines. Once God said, "Go, for I will deliver them into your hand." The second time the Lord said, "You shall *not* go . . . for the Lord has gone out before you to smite the army of the Philistines" (II Sam. 5:18–24). King Jehoshaphat was once instructed to take his position, stand still, and see the deliverance of the Lord . . . for the battle was not his, but God's. So instead of fighting, they sang songs of praise and won a mighty victory (II Chron. 20:14–26). I don't know how many times I have been out in the heat of some battle (sometimes involving the saints as well as Satan) getting battered and bruised—spiritually, emotionally, and physically—when the Lord would have had me singing praises on the sidelines while He corrected the situation in His own way. Sound familiar? Yes, we desperately need the ministry of self-protection!

6. PRAYER

The apostle Paul declares that when we are praying in the Spirit (our heavenly prayer language) we are being *edified* (I Cor. 14:4). The Greek word for "edify" is *oikodomeo* and means, literally, to "build a house." In general New Testament usage, it carries the added ideas of fortification, strength, improvement, and growth in spiritual character (inner man) which involves patient labor (ministry). In other words, praying in devotional tongues ministers to the spirit and soul of man. It is comforting to the heart and mind to know that the Holy Spirit can intercede on our behalf in perfect harmony with God's will (Rom. 8:26–27). He knows our needs better than do we ourselves, and can present our petitions with divine precision, when we don't even know what to pray for as we ought. Jude encourages us: "Build yourselves up . . . on your most holy faith—make progress, rise like an edifice higher and higher—*praying in the Holy Spirit*" (Jude 20 TAB, italics mine).

Praying in tongues (devotional prayer language) is for the purpose of praise, petition, intercession, and *self-edification.* There is nothing selfish or secondary about edifying ourselves, for only as we are built up in Christ can we be of service to others. We should take time every day for the express purpose of strengthening our inner man by praying in the Holy Spirit. When was the last time you specifically ministered to your inner self through spiritual prayer? It might be well to pause right now and allow God through His Holy Spirit of prayer to refresh your spirit and restore your soul.

There are many other ministries to the inner man which God can bring to your mind as it relates to His will for you. Our desire here is to establish the truth that there is a specific ministry to our inner selves for which we are responsible before God. If it is neglected, our service to the Body of Christ and witness to the world will be impaired. Self-edification as truly directed by the Holy Spirit will always enhance our ministry to others.

MINISTRY TO OTHERS

Ministry to others is not developed by choosing some particular vocation from a list, reading all the literature we can find on the subject, and moving forth as a self-styled servant of God. Nor is it something which is magically conferred upon a novice by the presumptuous laying on of hands. Occasionally such misconceptions have been promoted. A very sincere but spiritually immature Christian asked me the other day when her miracle ministry was going to begin. She had been in a meeting where a prophet of God had declared that everyone in the group was called to a miraculous ministry of spiritual power. Ill-chosen words had been sadly misinterpreted, and a bewildered handmaiden of God was at the point of being disillusioned; or worse yet, presumptuously moving forth under a delusion of grandeur, without the protection and counsel of a local Christian community. This is not to say that God may not on occasion use babes in Christ to accomplish real miracles in response to simple faith, but a ministry involves time, testing, and development within the context of a local fellowship.

On rare occasions, someone may receive a dramatic call, as did the apostle Paul, early in their Christian experience, but even he underwent an extensive and intensive time of preparation before his ministry fully matured. Usually ministries will emerge in the process of on-the-job-training experience as illustrated by Philip and Stephen (Acts 6:2–6; 8:5–8). There is something solid and sound about development which has the direction and loving concern which only a family relationship can bring. A teachable, submissive spirit will be unusually blessed of God in these days to come, for the Lord is restoring a divine order and authority to the Body of Christ. This is a theme which the Holy Spirit is emphasizing to the members of God's family everywhere.

The first prerequisite for discovering our ministry is to relate ourselves to a responsible local community or fellowship which recognizes charismatic ministries of the Holy Spirit. Ideally, this might be a local church or perhaps a mature prayer group composed of a variety of denominational backgrounds. The relation to the prayer group, however, should be more than casual. There needs to be a sense of loyalty, commitment, and submission to each other and the Lord. Spiritual leadership is to be recognized and appreciated.

Charismatic vitality and development can be found in home fellowship groups as described, but this does not preclude a witness and mutual ministry in a historic or denominational church as well, if God has placed us there. As long as we are so established in His will, we should submit to the authority of our spiritual leaders as unto the Lord. This doesn't mean they are always right, but it does allow the Lord to move in divine order concerning our witness and is a protection for us which the Lord will honor. There will be truth God will bring through them in spite of their limitations (and ours), and often such situations provide fertile ground in which the fruit of the Spirit can grow. The latter is one of the prime essentials in developing our ministry.

The second prerequisite for finding our function in Christ's Body is one of attitude. May we begin with the simple desire to share the life and love of Jesus with others as we have come to experience it in our own lives. We will trust the anointing of the Holy Spirit to freshly flow through our lives, touching every thought, word, and deed in such a way that people will be blessed to be around us. Common courtesies, thoughtful actions, and even a loving smile can be the beginning of our ministry of Jesus to others. We start with the people in our own world—at home, school, work, church, etc.

As we share the love of Jesus in little ways with those around us, larger opportunities will develop. Soon we will even be taking the initiative and creating situations where God can minister through our lives. We will be drawing deeply from the streams of the Spirit as we go, but initially it may be so naturally supernatural we won't even realize which fruit and gifts of the Spirit are being expressed. It is a ministry of truth in love, totally dependent on the Lord that the words we speak and the moves we make will reach the hearts and minds of those in need. Sometimes it is surprising how graciously God goes beyond our limitations when we are willing to simply minister His life in love.

As we go forth in faith, God will begin to bless our service for Him in some ways more than others. Certain gifts and fruit of the Spirit will become evident as the Lord begins to equip us for more defined ministry. With it will come a desire to be better prepared and assume the discipline and responsibility which that preparation will require. Furthermore, the brothers and sisters in our local fellowship will recognize and confirm the direction which God's Spirit is taking us in special service. No true prophet of God has to announce that he is a prophet.

The power and life of his ministry will authenticate his calling in a way which can be readily recognized by those in places of spiritual leadership and responsibility in the Body of Christ. The same is true for other ministries as well.

DIVERSITY OF MINISTRY

There is a great diversity of service in the family of God. Most of us are familiar with the previously mentioned fivefold ministry which God has given His church. Let us briefly review each one:

1. THE APOSTLE has a foundational, confirming, unifying, and informing trans-local ministry. Obviously there are no modern-day apostles in the unique sense with which we view the first Twelve. Apostolic functions, however, are just as essential now as ever. God has sovereignly raised up men with apostolic abilities whose spiritual ministries are universally recognized, although they may or may not hold an official title in a religious institution.

2. THE PROPHET uniquely moves the minds of men through a passionate (but not necessarily emotional) proclamation of what is on the heart and mind of God. He has a vision concerning God's will for the hour. His is a ministry of edification, exhortation, and consolation—build-up, stir-up and cheer-up (I Cor. 14:3).

3. THE EVANGELIST is equipped with the divine ability to clearly and convincingly present the Gospel of Christ in a manner which brings men to a place of decision.

4. THE PASTOR is one who has a shepherd's heart (and patience) and is concerned with the individual sheep and the welfare of the flock as a whole. His is a very practical ministry of direction, correction, and protection.

5. THE TEACHER has a love for God's Word, and the practical ways its truth can be translated into both individual

and corporate life. His desire is to understand God's will and the principles by which it can be achieved here on earth through the members of Christ's Body.

Other ministries are added from Paul's presentations found in Romans 12:6–8 and I Corinthians 12:28–29. They are listed in part as follows:

1. MINISTRY AND HELPS: This refers to practical service in the Body of Christ. It would include the office of deacon, but probably is much wider in scope. The emphasis is on practical activities rather than the spoken word.

2. EXHORTATION: This involves the elements of encouragement and admonition. One is reminded of Paul's exhortation to Timothy to stir up the gift that was resident within him (II Tim. 1:6–9). Faith is always stimulated by this ministry.

3. GIVING: The thought here relates to the idea of wisely contributing and sharing our earthly goods with simplicity (sincerity). There is no thought of condescension, reproach, or ulterior motive. A meaningful ministry is to be found in financial stewardship.

4. RULERSHIP AND GOVERNMENTS: Literally "to rule" means "to be placed in front." This is speaking of the role of leadership with diligence (earnest care) as an inherent quality. It also includes the element of concerned involvement (assistance) with those who are being led. This is in contrast to a kind of detached authority. The word "government" literally relates to guidance (pilotage). It involves the functions of administration, organization, and coordination in the Christian community. Very likely the office of elder (presbyter) is included in this category. Responsibility for the spiritual well-being of the community and the authority to wisely administrate that responsibility are involved.

5. MERCY: The ministry of mercy involves a feeling of sympathy for the needs of others, coupled with an adequate response which will meet that need. It is associated with a

cheerfulness (joyful eagerness) which makes such "glad angels of mercy" like unto "sunbeams penetrating a sick-chamber." Praise God for the ministry of mercy!

6. MIRACLES AND HEALING: We might group these two ministries under the heading of wonder-workers. These are unusual and often sensational "sign ministries." Their purpose is to point people to the reality of a present-tense God, who through His supernatural power desires not only to heal broken bodies but sin-scarred souls as well. A genuine miracle is a difficult argument to refute. It effectively prepares the way for a presentation of the Gospel. It also strengthens the faith of the saints. Of all ministries, these most need the protection and direction which the Body of Christ can provide.

This by no means exhausts the possibilities of ministry. Many others are implied throughout Scripture. A little reflection would add some of the following functions to our list:

1. INTERCESSORY PRAYER: Prayer and fasting is as important a ministry as some of the more obvious services for God. Many times after a great spiritual breakthrough I have felt that hidden prayers were being honored—perhaps of saints who have long-since won their rest.

2. HOSPITALITY: Many are the homes which have lovingly opened their doors to the stranger, traveling minister, the orphaned, and those lonely and oppressed. Surely He who had no place to rest His head appreciates such a personal and unselfish service of love (I Pet. 4:9).

3. VISITATION: Scriptures specifically state that the bereaved, the sick, the aged, and those imprisoned are of special concern to the Lord. We are informed that in visiting such as the least of these, we are ministering unto Him (Matt. 25:40).

4. SOCIAL CONCERN: In a broader sense, our concern for the poor and needy in our land should cause us to open our hands (and hearts) wide on their behalf (Deut. 15:11). Surely

there are wise, loving, yet aggressive Christians who can positively but persistently pursue the cause for social justice. Perhaps the freshest fruit and greatest gifts of the Spirit are needed for this ministry. Both motives and means can so easily be perverted without the safeguards of spiritual purpose and principle.

5. LITERATURE: The recorded word has always had a unique and important place in the history of God's people. The authority, power and influence of "it is written" cannot be calculated. The writing, publishing, and distribution of truly inspired literature is a ministry in this day of unusual witness which will surely invoke God's special blessing. The variety of expression can range from personal letters to scholarly treatises. What is truly touched by the Holy Spirit will possess a life that will leap to the heart and mind of the reader. Perhaps your heart leaps to the possibility of contributing to such a ministry.

6. COMMUNICATION—MODERN MEDIA: Advances in communication technology have provided a means of outreach almost beyond what we could have imagined a few years back. Sadly, Christians have usually lagged far behind the developing opportunities. Perhaps the Lord is calling pioneer ministries into being which will take advantage of and even anticipate the breakthroughs in this rapidly expanding field.

7. FINE ARTS: Music has always been a beautiful and powerful means of spiritual expression. God continues to refresh His people through this medium. The melody in our hearts is a gracious gift of the Spirit. Less appreciated by some traditions has been the ministry of the Spirit through the other art forms. In connection with the charismatic renewal, I have been impressed by the gracious manifestations of the Holy Spirit through the media of painting, crafts, banners, and even such diverse fields as architecture and sacred dance. In each

case, the artists and designers involved were not interested in art for art's sake, but art for the sake of God's glory. They prayerfully relied upon the creative attributes of the Holy Spirit, that their ministry would bring life to God's people, and enable them to worship the Lord with all that is within them. The fruit that followed confirmed God's blessing. Do you have a hidden talent which God desires developed as a ministry for His glory?

8. RECONCILIATION: The Scriptures declare there is a ministry of reconciliation (II Cor. 5:18). Basically, the thought is that of bringing others into harmony and peace with God. The vertical relationship, however, always entails a horizontal expression. Jesus said, "Blessed are the *peacemakers.*" Certainly this is a special ministry for our day, when the Father is in the process by His Spirit of making us one in Christ Jesus. This is more than just a mystical unity, for the world is to see something that will cause them to believe that Jesus really was sent into this world as the Prince of Peace. They may not be converted, but they will be confronted. All of us should contribute to this ministry, but some have an unusual blessing on their lives for ministering healing to the bruised Body of our Lord Jesus Christ. What a beautiful privilege it is to anoint His Body with the healing oil of God's love.

9. WORLD MISSIONS: Usually we think of mission fields geographically—in terms of foreign countries and nations. Missionaries are people who have the mission of sharing God's love and grace in Christ Jesus with those who have never heard the good news concerning their salvation. Missionary preparation involves learning the language and culture of the people to whom they are sent, that they might personally relate to them, earn their respect, and thereby gain a sympathetic hearing for God's message of love and redemption.

We can think of mission fields in another way, although the

same principles apply. Any group of people united by common interests, culture, and language comprise a field for missionary endeavor. They will respect and listen to someone who has earned their trust and respect. Often this is a person within their own group with whom they have been acquainted for some time. With this concept in mind, consider some of the following mission fields which are white unto harvest:

Family world	Medical world
Neighborhood	Political world
Business world	Military world
Academic world	Religious world
Athletic world	Ghetto world
Recreation world	Street-people world
Entertainment world	Teenage world
Fine Arts world	Senior-citizen world
Scientific world	And many others.

We all are citizens of one or more worlds and, therefore, missionary candidates by virtue of our affiliation. Jesus did say to go into all the world, beginning with our Jerusalem.

CONCLUSION

It is apparent that many ministries overlap, and any given individual may be involved in several complementary endeavors. Some appointments will have a diversity of expression, while others will be more specific and intense in direction. Furthermore, one function often becomes the foundation upon which another builds. Philip, the faithful *servant* (Acts 6:2–6), later became Philip the flaming *evangelist* (Acts 8:5–8).

All of us have a ministry and a mission field at hand. We begin where we are with what we have in the Lord. The school of the Spirit always involves on-the-job-training. The anointing of God's Spirit will provide the fruit and gifts of the Spirit necessary for our divine appointment. We are responsible, however, for cultivating the fruit and learning to excel in the expression of the gifts that we might become good and faithful servants of our Lord and Master Jesus Christ. Personal ministries are best discovered and developed within the encouragement and counsel of a local Spirit-filled fellowship. Every Spirit-baptized Christian has been anointed and appointed for God's glorious end-time purpose of unity within and witness without.

10

THE INFILLING AND OVERFLOWING
Refreshing Rivers

Ho! Everyone who *thirsts*, come to the waters; And you who have no money come, buy and eat. Come, buy wine and milk Without money and without cost. (Isa. 55:1 NASB)

For I will pour water upon him that is *thirsty*, and floods upon the dry ground: I will pour my Spirit upon your seed, and my blessing upon your offspring; and they will spring up like grass among the waters, as willows by the water courses. (Isa. 44:3–4 various versions)

Whoever drinks of the water I will give him shall never, no never, be *thirsty* any more. But the water I will give him shall become a spring of water *welling up* (flowing, bubbling) continually within him unto everlasting life. (John 4:14 TAB, modified)

Jesus stood forth and cried in a loud voice, If any man is *thirsty*, let him come to Me and drink! He who believes in Me as the Scripture has said, Out from his innermost being springs and rivers of living water shall continually *flow*. He was speaking here of the Holy Spirit, whom those who believed in Him were afterward to receive. For the Holy Spirit had not yet been given; because Jesus was not yet glorified. (John 7:37–39 TAB, modified)

And when the day of Pentecost was fully come, they were all assembled together in one place . . . and they were all *filled*—diffused throughout their souls—with the Holy Spirit and began to speak in other languages, as the Spirit gave them utterance. (Acts 2:1,4 various versions)

Then Peter, *filled* with the Holy Spirit, spake unto . . . [the] rulers of the people, and elders of Israel. . . . Now when they saw the boldness of Peter and John, and perceived they were untrained laymen, they were astonished and realized they had been with Jesus. (Acts 4:8,13 various versions)

And now, Lord, behold their threats and enable your servants *full* freedom to fearlessly speak your word. . . . And when they had prayed, their meeting place was shaken, and they were all *filled* with the Holy Spirit and spoke the word of God boldly. (Acts 4:29,31 various versions)

Wherefore, brethren, select from among yourselves seven men of good report, *full* of the Holy Spirit and wisdom, whom we will assign to this business. . . . And they selected Stephen, a man *full* of faith and the Holy Spirit. . . . Now Stephen, *full* of grace and power, did great wonders and miracles among the people. (Acts 6:3,5,8 various versions)

The Jews stirred up the most respected and religious women and the chief men of the city and instigated persecution against Paul and Barnabas and drove them out of the district . . . leaving their converts, however, *filled* with joy and the Holy Spirit. (Acts 13:50,52 various versions)

May God, the fountain of hope, so *fill* you with perfect joy and peace through your continuing faith that, through the power of the Holy Spirit, you may be *overflowing* (*bubbling over*) with hope. (Rom. 15:13 various versions)

And that hope never disappoints us, for God's love *floods* our hearts through the Holy Spirit which has been given to us. (Rom. 5:5 various versions)

Do not drink wine to excess which leads to dissipation, but be *filled* with (drink deeply of) the Spirit; your tongues unloosed in psalms, hymns and spiritual songs, offering praise with your voices and making melody in your heart to the Lord. (Eph. 5:18–19 various versions)

As the hart panteth after the water brooks, so panteth my soul after thee, O God. My soul *thirsteth* for God, for the living God: when shall I come and appear before God? (Ps. 42:1–2)

Then He showed me the river whose waters give life, sparkling like crystal, *flowing* out from the throne of God and of the Lamb. . . . "Come!" say the Spirit and the bride. "Come!" let each hearer reply. Come forward, you who are *thirsty;* accept the water of life, a free gift to all who desire it. (Rev. 22:1,17 TAB and NEB)

As the Hart Panteth After the Water Brooks

While in college, I spent two summers working for the United States Forest Service as a lookout fireman in the Cascade Mountains of eastern Oregon. Early in the fire season, before the humidity dropped to a level which necessitated manning the fire-towers, we were responsible for checking out the service roads in the back country. Fallen trees and other obstacles had to be cleared away to insure ready access by the mobile units should a fire develop in these remote areas. It was most invigorating to head out into the hills in the early morning as the warm, golden rays of the rising sun gradually descended along the slopes of the surrounding mountains to the shaded valleys below. As the brisk breezes of the night gave way to the warmer winds of the morning, the temperature would begin to noticeably rise in its race with the sun.

Dusty roads, pine sawdust, and salty sweat have a way of creating an intense thirst as the heat of the day increases. There is always lukewarm water in the canteens, but dry throats and flushed faces are hopeful of a more satisfying solution. And what a welcome sight it is to round a corner and suddenly see before you a rough log bridge under which is rushing a sparkling, snow-fed mountain stream. Crystal pools of icy cold water, bordered by the fragrant ferns and moist mosses found on the streamside, extend an invitation for refreshment which prompts an immediate response. Little thought is given to dignity as one scrambles to the water's edge, stretches out full-length, and drinks deep drafts of the clear, cool water. There is no other earthly satisfaction that can quite compare.

The Psalmist must have experienced similar times of intense thirst while tending his sheep in the Palestinian pastures. In reaching for an earthly parallel to describe his deep desire for God, he draws upon a vivid figure of speech. "As the hart panteth after the water brooks, so panteth my soul after thee!" (Ps. 42:1). The yearning and longing of his soul could be expressed in no other way. Such has been the cry of men and women throughout the ages who have sought the Lord with all their hearts. Sometimes it is most beneficial for us to develop a deep hunger and thirst for God, for with it grows a great appreciation for His gracious provision. It is a safeguard against indifference and presumption.

Perhaps many of us can identify with the heart-cry of the Psalmist. I remember a promise from the prophets which came to mean very much to me when I was seeking the reality of Holy Spirit Baptism: "And ye shall seek me, and find me, when ye shall search for me with all your heart" (Jer. 29:13). Intense longing for God has a very purifying effect upon our values and goals in life. Furthermore, the Lord is aware of our heart's desire, for He set it there Himself when we surrendered our heart to Him. All through Scripture we are assured that those who thirst shall indeed be satisfied.

FILLED TO OVER- AND EVER-FLOWING

The familiar story of our Lord's unusual invitation to those who thirst after the water of everlasting life is worthy of our consideration (John 7:37–39). The occasion for His rather startling statement involved the final and climaxing day of the Feast of Tabernacles. This annual festival was celebrated in memory of God's provision and protection during Israel's wilderness wanderings. During the week-long feast, they built temporary tabernacles or booths, with branches of palm trees and willows symbolizing the divine shelter which the Lord provided for their families. Because it was held after the final harvest of fruit and grain, it was also called the Feast of Ingathering. It was a festival time, filled with joy and praise. Daily sacrifices of bullocks, rams, and lambs with their prescribed meat and drink offerings were a part of the ceremonial ritual.

One phase of ceremonial activity was especially significant in light of our Lord's aforementioned invitation. Early every morning a priest, followed by a joyous musical procession, went down to the nearby pool of Siloam and drew water into a golden pitcher. Upon their return to the temple, the priest brought the water to the altar and poured it into a silver basin with holes in the bottom which allowed the water to drain onto the altar. The congregation accompanied the ceremony by singing the Hallel (Ps. 113–118). On the eighth and last day of the feast, the water ritual was not performed; instead, the people beat the altar with branches and boughs. Undoubtedly they were reminded of the rock struck by Moses in the wilderness which provided for them a river of fresh-flowing, life-giving water. Probably the ceremony also symbolized their continuing prayer for water, since their agricultural economy was totally dependent upon the former and latter rains. This last day of the feast was indeed the greatest day of all. It concluded not only the Feast of Tabernacles, but the entire cycle of the festal year as well.

Perhaps Jesus was somewhat saddened by all the attention and activity related to the elaborated rituals when He, who was the fulfillment of all that the ceremonies symbolized, was unrecognized in their midst. He took the occasion once again to point them to the reality their rituals represented. Standing in a place of prominence, He loudly and clearly cried out, "If any man thirst, let him come unto me and drink!" (John 7:37). The people fell silent, acutely aware that He was directing their attention to something far more significant than that which could be obtained at the Pool of Siloam. "He that believes in me as the Scriptures have said, out of his innermost being shall flow rivers of living water!" (John 7:38 various versions).

At this point in the record, John cannot restrain himself from interpreting the meaning of Christ's words. He was living on this side of Pentecost, and he knew personally and experientially what the streams were of which Jesus spoke. Therefore he comments as follows: "He (Jesus) referred to the Spirit which they that believe on Him were about to receive, for the Holy Spirit had not yet come because Jesus had not yet been raised to glory" (John 7:39 various versions). John makes it very clear that the streams of living water were to be the expressions of the Holy Spirit Himself as He released the life of Jesus in us. The Spirit of Christ is sometimes referred to in Elizabethan English as the Holy Ghost. The term, "Ghost," is not a bad choice, for the word literally means the spirit of one who has *departed,* but *returned* to make his presence known! Again the lovely mystery of the Trinity is seen from a little different perspective. The life-giving streams of the Spirit are also Christ-revealing and Christ-releasing rivers—to and through us.

CONTINUITY AND DIVERSITY

Two important aspects to our life in the Spirit might be characterized by the terms *continuity* and *diversity*. Let us consider the concept of continuity first. Our spiritual flight-pattern should look like that of the mighty eagle sweeping onward and upward as we mount higher and higher into the heavens. Actually, we may wobble a little as we go, since we are human and have our ups and downs, but the net result is always in one direction—heavenward. The members of the first Christian community illustrate the idea, for they were described as *continuing* "*stedfastly* in the apostles' doctrine and fellowship, and in breaking of bread, and in prayers" (Acts 2:42).

I was reading the comic strip "Peanuts" one day, laughing at the very erratic flight-pattern of the little bird, Woodstock. He always enters the picture flying in circles or upside down in a great display of instability. Maybe you don't think the Lord reads the funny papers, but I am almost sure I heard Him say, "Does that look familiar?" Sadly, our spiritual airborne maneuvers sometimes assume a similar pattern.

Jesus indicated in His call to those who thirst what the secret is for the filled-to-over-and-ever-flowing life. His invitation to come to Him in our time of need calls for obedience on our part. If we move in some other direction—*within* to our feelings and reason, or *without* to circumstances or worldly counsel—we grieve the indwelling Holy Spirit, and the flow of life will slacken. Furthermore, our coming to Jesus must be in steadfast faith. In the tenses of the original language, Christ's words might be paraphrased as follows: "He that *continually* believes in me as the Scripture has said, out of his innermost being shall *continually* flow rivers of living water" (John 7:38 various versions). In other words, faith and obedience are the keys to the overflowing life. Doubt and disobedience will bottle-up the living water and stem its life-giving flow.

"Living water" was an Oriental idiom for what we would refer to as freshly flowing, running water. As Jesus finds His place in our hearts as the Lord of our lives, He becomes to us an interior fountain of everlasting satisfaction. Only the spontaneous springs of the Spirit can satisfy the inner longings of the soul for the many expressions of God's grace. Worldly fountains of pleasure, power, or prestige will never quench man's thirst for eternal life. The abundant life that Jesus promised is possible only as we in faith and obedience respond to His love and submit to Him as Savior and Baptizer. In this transaction, the Holy Spirit, as the Spirit of Christ, indwells us and fills us to overflowing with the rivers of divine life and power.

We must come (obedience to Christ's word) and we must drink (belief in Christ's word) before the streams will start to flow. In one sense, *Jesus* is the "indwelling fountain," and the many *manifestations of the Spirit* are the overflowing rivers of living water. This brings us to a discussion of the second concept involved in the passage—the diverse qualities which are inherent in our life in Christ.

Jesus promised that our faith in His Word would release rivers of living water—streams of the Spirit—from our innermost being. The use of the plural indicates we should expect a variety of expression regarding this ministry of Christ's life by the Holy Spirit. As we shall see, this provides the practical basis by which we can be ever-filled to overflowing. If we are perfectly honest, we may have held the concept of "continuity" (ever-flowing) as a little idealistic, even though in our heads we recognized it should work in principle. It was this companion concept of "diversity" which helped me to understand that the *ideal* could be progressively *realized* in our daily lives.

THE RAINBOW OF LIFE

Jesus is the light of the world. Through the revealing ministry of the Holy Spirit, the divine light of God's love and truth is to flood our lives in a brilliant display of His glory. This is more than poetic language; it is the very purpose of our existence.

> Once you were all darkness, but now you are all light in the Lord: walk (live and act) as children of light. For the fruit of the Spirit (product of light) may be seen in every shade of goodness, righteousness and truth. Let your lives be living proof of what is pleasing to God. (Eph. 5:8–10 various versions)

> You are all children of the light and sons of the day . . . therefore let us who belong to daylight control ourselves, putting on the breastplate of faith and love, with the hope of salvation as our helmet. (I Thess. 5:5,8 various versions)

> You are the light of the world. . . . Let your light shine before men that they may see the beauty of your life and glorify your Father which is in heaven. (Matt. 5:14,16 various versions)

As pure white light is broken by a prism into the many colors of the rainbow, so the light of Jesus is to so radiate from our lives that the many qualities of His life are distinctly displayed in a world which is spiritually dark and colorless. The many streams of the Spirit represent the rainbow colors of Christ's life as they are expressed in the diversity of fruit and gifts. The various manifestations of the Holy Spirit are expressions of the different qualities of Christ's life and character. All are needed in the Body of Christ, or something of His beauty and authority is diminished.

The fruit of the Spirit demonstrates Christ's character (being). The I AM of God takes on added meaning as we realize that Jesus was not just a loving, joyful, peaceful person;

but HE IS *love*, HE IS *joy* and HE IS *peace*. All the other fruit of the Spirit (Gal. 5:22–23) could be defined in like fashion: long-suffering (patience), gentleness (kindness), goodness (benevolence), faith (faithfulness), meekness (humility), and temperance (self-control). These are word-pictures which describe the character of Jesus in living color.

To be conformed into the image of Jesus also involves the expression of the gifts of the Spirit (I Cor. 12:4–12). The list in the Corinthian letter is typical of the qualities which are necessary if we are to think, speak, and act as Jesus did. In fact they can be categorized as thought, word, and deed gifts:

1. THOUGHT-REALM GIFTS: knowledge, wisdom, discernment
2. WORD-REALM GIFTS: tongues, interpretation, prophecy
3. DEED-REALM GIFTS: faith, healings, miracles

These streams of the Spirit are also essential for a full demonstration of Christ's life. If any are neglected in the Body of Christ, some of the colors in the rainbow will be missing.

It becomes apparent that there is a great diversity of spiritual ministry which is to flow through our lives. Furthermore, which combinations of streams and their intensity of flow will vary from time to time depending upon our needs and God's purpose.

VARIATIONS ON A THEME

It was this understanding concerning diversity and variety in the overflowing life which brought me out from under an attitude of failure and condemnation. I had unconsciously equated the fullness of the Spirit with a feeling of joy or sometimes the opposite extreme—a broken spirit. Both are streams of the Spirit, but there are many more. God's great theme of life has many variations.

Have you ever been in a meeting where there was a great deal of joy, blessing, and enthusiasm, but you felt like a lead ball on the inside, and secretly hoped nobody would ask you to pray? Even showers of blessing can be annoying when they are falling on everybody but you.

Dark clouds of resentment and self-condemnation can be quickly dispelled if we immediately confess the blessing of God's forgiveness, should our attitude require this, and then allow the Lord to sort out which streams are most appropriate for His present purpose in our lives. Perhaps it will be the river of peace or rest. We can't always live on a high crest of emotion, even in meetings of unusual blessing. Sometimes God may desire from us the stream of intercessory prayer on behalf of those who are responding with much joy and enthusiasm—a petition that they will remain steadfast in faith and persist in the new direction into which God has moved them after the emotional element fades away. The Lord can reset our lives by reaching our hearts, but it takes a commitment to the truth to maintain a steady pace in God's will.

Some situations demand a flow of love and wisdom far beyond our own capacity, if we are a little weary and worn ourselves, but this is what the streams of the Spirit are for. We don't always need to feel tip-top in order for God to do a first-rate work of grace through our lives if we are in His will. I have seen the Holy Spirit bring forth some rather lively ministry when as the minister, I felt half-dead physically. On other occasions, the Lord's will for me was to rest in Him and allow the refreshing rivers of His Spirit to restore my soul, while others were perhaps more expressive in their worship and ministry.

Even in times of distress and discouragement, when we feel nothing but depressed, we can still be filled to overflowing. It may not be the stream of exuberant joy, but there can be a flow of faith and wisdom concerning God's will and future purpose. I doubt if Paul was singing the "Hallelujah Chorus" when he was being beaten with forty stripes save one. I am convinced he was filled with long-suffering, forgiveness, and determination. That is the overflowing life. Our joy is not in our feelings or circumstances, but in the Lord who assured us He would never leave us nor forsake us.

There is a tremendous truth taught in Scripture which indicates that the finest fruit of the Spirit is grown from the opposing ground of natural circumstances. The apostle Paul informed the Lord he was being significantly limited by his thorn in the flesh, and implied he was quite sure God didn't want his ministry to be handicapped by anything of such an adverse nature. After running his prayer through three times—with some intensity of feeling—Paul heard the Lord reply that He planned to answer his prayer far beyond his expectations. Instead of removing the thorn, He was going to cultivate the ground of Paul's weakness that He might perfect in him His very own strength (II Cor. 12:7–10).

God can always limit and redeem evil for His good purposes. He will work all things together that the fine fruit of the Spirit will be produced in our lives. Nothing can ever touch us that the Holy Spirit cannot use to make us more like Jesus. Out of the natural ground of sadness, turmoil, and irritation, God can bring forth His joy, peace, and patience. Our natural desire is to race through our shadowed valleys so quickly we miss the banquet table with its fine fruit and gracious gifts.

God will blend the fruit and gifts of His Spirit in just the proper proportions for Him to fulfill His purpose in and through our lives. We would like a perpetual arrangement of love, joy, and peace; but faith, wisdom, and patience make a complementary chord which harmonizes well during the stresses and demands of life. The important thing is not to limit the Lord in the variety of combinations He would wisely choose. Once more we are reminded that the *nature* and *intensity* of the spiritual streams may vary greatly, but we can always be filled to overflowing regardless of feelings or circumstances.

CHARISMATIC PERSONALITIES

It would be interesting to make a character study of some of the charismatic personalities whom God used in establishing the early New Testament church. They faced a variety of unusual obstacles, but as they moved with the flow of God's Spirit and allowed the streams to flow through them, nothing could hold back the tide of life that flooded the then-known world. The Book of Acts might have been titled, *The Streams of the Spirit*, for each life became a fountain filled to overflowing. They relied upon the fruit and gifts of the Spirit to accomplish their task, and the Scriptures relate they turned the world upside down.

The life of Jesus, of course, is the most perfect example of what the charismatic Christian should be like. It would be most profitable to thoroughly examine some of the incidents in His earthly ministry for obvious expressions of the spiritual fruit and gifts. He was totally dependent upon the Holy Spirit to fulfill the will of His Father, and thereby pioneered the way for us concerning our witness to the world.

> Then Jesus went back full of and under the power of the (Holy) Spirit into Galilee, and the fame of Him spread through the whole region round about. (Luke 4:14 TAB)

> And you shall receive power after the Holy Spirit has come upon you and you shall be my witnesses in Jerusalem, in all Judea, and in Samaria and unto the uttermost part of the earth. (Acts 1:8 various versions)

The noun "witness" refers to someone who will furnish evidence based on personal experience. It is derived from the Greek word *martus* from which we also get the English term "martyr." The early Christians bore witness to something so real they were willing to die for it. Even physical death couldn't stifle the stream of spiritual life which would forever flow from their eternal relationships with Jesus Christ. A saint was once asked if he had "dying" grace. "No," he replied, "but I expect to when the time comes!" His confidence was in the indwelling Christ who is the fountainhead from which all of God's graces spring forth. Such can be our assurance as well—for the demands of life as well as death—because the wellspring of God's love forever abides within our hearts.

THE RIVER OF LIFE

The different phases of our life in the Spirit can be studied by comparing them with the life story of a natural river as it is followed from its inception on a high mountain peak to its final destination in the vast ocean below. The character of the river changes significantly along its course and corresponds to the variety of spiritual experiences which are a part of our developing life in Christ. Such an approach keeps us from putting God into a stereotyped pattern and thereby provides the latitude necessary for the Holy Spirit to move with freedom in our lives. As we follow the river along, some phases will appeal to us more than others, but to some extent we need to be acquainted with every part of the entire course if we are to have a truly balanced life. Let us consider our story one phase at a time.

New Born Streamlets

For months the high mountain country has been softly covered by blanket after blanket of white wintery snow. The ground is frozen hard, and jagged icicles fringe the rocky ledges. As the warm springtime sun ascends higher each day into the azure sky, the silvery silence of winter gradually gives way to the happy sounds of nature as she gently awakens a sleeping world. Mighty masses of ice slowly surrender to the persistent testimony of the tiny sunbeam, and the tinkling notes of falling water-drops fill the air with a lovely melody— of a music-box-like quality, but more exquisite than anything produced by the hand of man. Little insignificant streamlets— freshly born—now add their happy song as they obey nature's call to follow their downward course. They are moving toward a goal far greater than could ever have been anticipated from such a simple origin. We have just described the birth of what someday will be a mighty flowing river.

The Song of Solomon may be considered as a beautiful allegory concerning the love relationship between the Lord and His people. At one point in the story, the bride is described as one "that looketh forth as the morning, fair as the moon, clear as the sun, and terrible as an army with banners" (Song of Sol. 6:10). The attributes of God's people are derived from the gracious ministries of the Holy Spirit which enable us to be transformed into His glorious image (II Cor. 3:18).

The little phrase, "clear as the sun," speaks of its bright warm rays which possess both a revealing and a melting power. Divine truth can reveal God's grace to our minds, while divine love can melt our hearts with His goodness. How faithful the Holy Spirit was to reveal to us our sin and then show us the way to our Savior. Even when our heads were hard and our hearts were cold, God's sunbeams of love and truth persistently melted away our resistance that we might have an opportunity to begin a new way of life—an abundant life with Him—that will last forever. Can we be as patient and persistent with others as the Lord has been with us? Should we not be so overflowing with His life that others will ever see

Jesus in us and even get wet with the warm streams of His love when they get close to us—and we get close to them?

The more I grow in God's grace, the more I appreciate the overcoming power there is in living the truth in love. One of the sterling qualities about the love of God is related to patience and long-suffering. It takes more than a day for the winter's accumulation of ice and snow to be converted into rivers of life-giving water, yet we sometimes expect hearts hardened by years of disappointment, bitterness, resentment, and rebellion to be melted overnight. It is true, God can accelerate the springtime process of salvation in the lives of those prepared by our love and prayers. In Alaska, after the spring breakup of winter-long ice and snow, they experience an almost instant spring. Everything leaves out in a matter of days. It can happen. On the other hand, sometimes the sunbeams meant for others get filtered out if there are dark, cold areas in our own lives which we are reluctant to submit to the melting power of God's love and truth. Once we do, we can make a grand discovery; the same divine rays that released us can release others if they too are willing to submit. Sometimes our submission paves the way for theirs. Only after we have gone this far ourselves should we expect anything more from others.

This does not mean that eventually everyone will yield to the Lord in spite of their will, for God does not violate the sovereignty of our lives. It does mean that exposure to the Light will bring one to a place of freedom to choose. To willfully and persistently retreat to the darkness is most serious, for in the sunless shadows one can be chilled into a state of fatal indifference. The decisions which we face in this life will determine our destiny in the next. God will faithfully honor our choice in time for eternity. This not only involves our salvation, but our discipleship as well. Both our conversation and conduct will be exposed to the motive-revealing light of God's justice. If we joyfully submit to that light now, we will joyfully submit to it then!

> Here, then, is the message which we heard from him: GOD IS LIGHT, and no shadow of darkness can exist in him. Consequently, if we were to say that we enjoyed fellowship with him and still went on living in darkness, we should be both telling and living a lie. But if we really are living in the same light in which he eternally exists, then we have true fellowship with each other, and the blood which his Son shed for us keeps us clean from all sin. (I John 1:5–7 Phillips)

May we never underestimate the melting power which the sunbeams of God's love can exert upon the lives of our loved ones. Let us ever be aglow with the beautiful Spirit of our Savior. Springtime may be sooner than we think!

The Merry Mountain Brook

A thousand silvery streamlets sing their way along in joyful expectation, for soon they will blend their voices in happy harmony as they join the matchless music of the merry mountain brook. The laughing, splashing waters seem to be rippling with anticipation as they gaily rush over the rounded rocks of the fast-falling streambed on its way to the mountain meadow below. Wayward water drops sparkle brilliantly against the dark shadows of the ravine as shafts of early morning sunlight highlight the antics of our river-in-the-making. There is a joyful enthusiasm to be found in the freshness and freedom displayed by the little brook as it hurries happily along. It has been a long, dark, frigid winter, but now the atmosphere is alive with hope and expectation, for spring has come at last. All nature hears the call to throw off the restraint of the past season and embrace the promise for new life. No wonder our mountain brook has such a merry song!

For, lo, the winter is past, the rain is over and gone; The flowers appear on the earth, the time of singing of birds is come, and the voice of the turtledove is heard in our land. The fig tree puts forth . . . her green figs, and the vines are in blossom; they give forth their fragrance. Arise, my love, my fair one, and come away. (Song of Sol. 2:11–13 TAB)

How beautifully this phase in the life-cycle of our river characterizes the fresh feelings of joy and enthusiasm which we find in our new life relationship with Jesus. There is an exhilarating sense of hope and expectation much as described in the Song of Solomon by the little phrase, "that looketh forth as the morning." With the dawn of eternal life is a positive attitude which is fresh with promise for the new day. The little chorus, "In My Heart There Rings a Melody," rises readily to our lips from the wellsprings of our heart. Life has a bright, new feeling that sometimes is too good to believe.

Often such feelings are also associated with the release which God's Spirit brings to our lives from some bondage from the past. We breathe deeply the fresh, life-giving air of freedom, and with it we find ourselves spontaneously praising God over and over again for His goodness. Life has a new sense of direction and purpose, and we, indeed, greet each day with anticipation and enthusiasm. God has put a new song in our hearts, and we are eager to press forward into the future which is filled with faith and bright hope.

Most of us would be quite content to picnic along this portion of the streamside forever. Everything is so happy and gay, and there isn't a solitary cloud in the sky. The Lord has wiser plans, however, and we shall discover He is more interested in putting the stream in us, than in our parking along its edge. The abiding, indwelling joy of the Lord is ever to be our strength, but there are other ministries of the Spirit as well—some designed for maturity and growth that will enable us to remain faithful, regardless of our feelings. As we follow our mountain stream along, we will find to our initial dismay that the entire scene is about to change.

The Underground Stream

The downward course of the mountain brook was toward the open meadow. Before reaching the base of our rocky slope, we are bewildered to see our stream slacken its lively flow and eventually disappear into the rocks and sand of a narrow ravine. The happy sounds of the merry brook are replaced by the dusty silence of a dry riverbed. How could something that began so beautifully suddenly disappear, leaving in its path nothing but disappointment? We should have known it was too good to last. Sadness is mixed with frustration, and even resentment.

How often this is a picture of our life in the Lord. The fresh flow of joy and enthusiasm slows to a trickle, and sometimes seems to dry up completely as far as feelings and circumstances are concerned. In milder moments, we wistfully recall the good old days and wish we could recapture the happy hours that so richly blessed our spiritual childhood. Fellowship had been so exciting; we could have lived forever in such pleasant company. (Sometimes it was the wee hours of the morning before the prayer meeting was over.) We had been warned the honeymoon wouldn't last forever, but we hadn't expected the bridegroom to leave us completely alone—or so it seems.

I opened to my beloved, but my beloved had turned away and withdrawn himself, and was gone! My soul went forth to him when he spoke, but it failed me, and now he was gone! I sought him, but I could not find him; I called him, but he gave me no answer. (Song of Sol. 5:6 TAB)

There is a time when God calls us beyond our happy feeling about Him, to Himself alone. There comes the privilege of worshiping the Lord, not because He makes us feel good, but because He is always faithful and ever worthy. Though the valley be dark and our Shepherd unseen, we will not fear, for He is with us, even though there is no confirming evidence—other than His Word.

On occasion, the stream of God's Spirit will seemingly move underground, but its life-giving flow is still there, though unseen. After our faith has been tried, and we have matured, fresh streams will again break forth with evident grace. God will never allow us to be tempted beyond what we are able to bear, but the added weight of trial will strengthen our faith and dedication. Every great saint of God can point to the dry streambeds in his past, and confess they were filled with divine purpose. Therefore, we are not to be surprised, but understanding, when such times come.

As we mature in the Lord, He will often wait for us in faith to sink a well ourselves, and discover the stream is just below the very ground upon which we walk. There have been distinct times when I have felt God wanted me to make a move in faith and obedience, rather than impatiently wait for the Spirit to suddenly surface in my situation of distress. Many of the suggestions given earlier in the book concerning ways to appropriate healing and deliverance were really techniques for digging wells.

The companion concepts of God's sovereign provision and man's responsible endeavor in faith are presented in the following passage:

> Blessed is the man whose strength is in the Lord, in whose heart are the highways to Zion. Passing through the barren valley of weeping they make it a place of springs; the early rain also fills it with pools of refreshing. They grow stronger as they go; each of them will see the Lord in Zion. (Ps. 84:5–7 various versions)

Winding Streams in Mountain Meadows

The underground stream surfaces as the mountain meadow is reached. Its character now changes to accommodate the rounded contours of the open field. The babbling brook which hurried its way down the hillside is transformed into a silent, slow-moving stream which winds from one side of the meadow to the other as it seriously searches out the direction for its future course. As the stream is strengthened by the soft spring rains and converging tributaries from the surrounding hills, it moves ever more swiftly to the edge of the meadow where yet another drastic change is expected. It is as if it has found its calling and with renewed force now rushes to its destiny.

The underground-stream experiences in our lives are always enriching, for they develop an appreciation for God's presence and a desire to abide in His will and favor. No longer are blessings an end in themselves, but a means of reinforcing His purpose for our lives. As we move about seeking our place in the Lord, we endeavor to be sensitive to the guiding touch of His Holy Spirit. We are no longer interested in rushing merrily along without defined goals, for we are anxious to redeem the time in effective ministry. Sometimes it would seem our course is more trial-and-error than we would desire, but we discover it is as important to understand why God says no, as why He says yes. In the process, we become better acquainted with Him and ourselves. A sense of divine destiny develops, and we become motivated more by defined purpose than by our fluctuating feelings, and/or capricious circumstances. Our ministry begins to develop, and we are ready to move forth with force and faith. Boldly then, we come to the edge of our maturing-meadow experience and are ready for our next phase of active ministry for the Lord.

A Cascading Waterfall

The swollen meadow stream now moves with force and direction onward to the edge of the meadow. A dramatic phase of our river-cycle now suddenly begins, for the boundary of the meadow forms the leap-over edge of a mighty precipice. With the surging power of a rushing river, one mighty leap is made into space, and cascading streams of water fall with a sustained roar upon the ragged rocks below. The sights and sounds are spectacular: angry, white water churning full-force in the basin below; splash and spray sparkling like diamonds thrown wildly into the air; and the whole setting framed by the rainbow-colored mists set aflame by the morning sun. What could be more important in the course of a river than such a dramatic display as this? Surely there is no need to follow on for further understanding, since here we have the finest expression of beauty and power which one could ever hope to see. How we wish it were possible to be forever immersed in the magic of the moment, but the rushing water is about to carry us on to an unexpected consequence.

There are miraculous ministries of the Holy Spirit which are nothing short of sensational. One is reminded how God's people are to be characterized as "an army terrible with banners!" Fantastic expressions of God's power and glory run throughout the Lord's earthly ministry. Dramatic healings with tender touches of personal beauty were frequently recorded in the Gospels. Spectacular displays of resurrection power occurred several times over; yet in each case, miracles and wonder-works were never allowed to become ends in themselves. They were necessary signs which pointed to the Man and His message, wherein lay divine purpose and eternal life. Miracles healed sick bodies, and were the credentials of divinity; but only Christ's words of forgiveness could cleanse man's immortal soul and set his spirit free.

Many of Christ's followers wanted a steady diet of miracles and were frankly disinterested in His message of discipleship. They soon forsook His ministry altogether, for they were more interested in Kingdom power than in the King. God's power must never be divorced from His purpose. Both are essential for His will to be accomplished here on earth through His people. The Enemy would subtly deceive us into emphasizing one without the other. Waterfall Christians are prone to stress divine power over purpose, and miracles over message. There are consequences, however, which become obvious as we consider what happens next in the life story of our river.

Whirlpools and Riverside Eddies

Below the waterfall, a narrow rocky gorge channels the churning waters into a roaring river which flexes its rippling muscles in defiance toward any obstacle which would dare to impede its progress. Indeed, so forceful is its flow it seems no barrier could ever withstand the surging power of our mighty, onrushing river. Downstream, however, the riverbed broadens, and large boulders divert the charging waters into separate currents which conflict with each other as they continually converge and diverge in a most contrary way. Along the riverside, large whirlpools are formed which relentlessly rotate, as counter-currents effectively restrain any effort for release to the mainstream of flow.

I recall watching with fascination a whirlpool situation along the rocky riverbed of the Spokane River in the state of Washington. A log had been captured by the swirling waters and was endlessly rotating within its riverside prison. It would repeatedly swing one end into the mainstream of flow and appear to have won its freedom, but a strong counter-current just a little way beyond would bring the log back under the relentless power of the whirling waters. It was a spellbinding scene from which it was difficult to tear oneself away. Even though the outcome was always the same, I kept thinking maybe next time a more favorable angle of entrance by the log back into the mainstream would allow it to break away from the sinister power of the contrary currents. It would appear many times to have succeeded, when hidden watery fingers would once more frustrate its attempt to be free, and the familiar pattern would begin all over again. The poor log was battered and scarred by the repeated encounters with the rocky walls of its prison. It was a very vivid scene which I will never forget.

The application is almost too obvious (and painful) for some of us to pursue. Anyone with activist tendencies will recognize this river scene without any difficulty. There can be a relentless, driving desire to be where the action is. If anything is happening, we have got to be there—in fact, it might not happen if we aren't. Now there is an important and necessary place in God's plan for both spectacular waterfalls and churning white waters as we shall see; but the Deceiver ever desires to take the miracle-ministries of God and through unbalanced extremism ultimately pervert the power and purpose for which they were given.

It is possible to wear ourselves (and others) out in our work for the Lord. We can push and promote our ministry with such force that the Holy Spirit steps aside, and we come under the control of all kinds of contrary currents. There is an initial delusion to whirlpool activity. The action of churning water, the exhilaration of much movement, blinds us from the fact that we aren't going anywhere—but in circles. Actually, God does bless anything we do in His name as much as He can; but we are talking about the diminishing returns and ultimate consequences of uncontrolled effort which many times involve worldly methods.

How important it is as we mature, to define our responsibilities for ministry, and establish our priorities before God.

Otherwise our families, friends, and the local Christian community suffers as we dissipate our energies by assuming a diversity of tasks the Lord never intended for us. One of my most difficult decisions is to say no in the name of Jesus. The Lord had to discipline me to my desk to get this book written. It is so easy to go dashing off on another assignment, even though it violates the priorities God has set. If we do, the Lord's full blessing will be withheld, and we may find red flags waving in some area of our ministry, health, finances, or family. If we will be sensitive and obedient to His voice, however, the power of God's Spirit can restore us once again to the mainstream of His will for our lives. As He does, we will discover another dimension in our walk with God which is seen in the next phase of river life.

The Reflecting Pool

The frenzy of rapid waters is replaced by a more tranquil scene as our river broadens, slows its pace, and more leisurely explores the quiet deeps of the riverside. As a boy I used to swim and fish in the Washougal River in the hill country of Washington. Many of the pictures in my mind as I write are derived from streamside experiences in the forested region I roamed in my earlier years. There is a fall on the Washougal River which is very beautiful. Below the fall, the river rushes fiercely through a deep, narrow gorge, which ultimately widens into a broad, shallow basin that forms the borders of a placid pool of restful water. The contrast is striking, for the scene changes rather quickly from turbulence to tranquillity. The still surface of the water mirrors the blue heavens and fleecy clouds above, and occasionally a lazy leaf will drift slowly by as if reluctant to leave such a peaceful place of repose. A wooden bridge arches across the lovely pool, and its shade provides a restful setting for reflection and quiet meditation.

The healing powers of nature are needed for weary bodies, burned-out minds, and spent emotions. Still waters and green pastures were designed to restore the soul of man, and we desperately need to come aside and "rest awhile" with the Lord. There is a place in God which enables us to become as fair as the moon. Our lives should be as refreshing to others as a calm summer evening after a noisy day in the sultry marketplace. The bright light of the blazing sun is replaced by the soft shadows of the moonlight night, and a spirit of repose brings a sweet serenity of soul. It is in the peaceful reflection of the evening quiet-hour that God can restore our inner composure and whisper words of reassurance.

We many times complain because God doesn't speak to us, when in truth we are so busy and noisy in earthly affairs and efforts (often for the Lord) that we don't have time or the ear to hear His voice. Yet it is during our quiet-times apart with the Lord that we find refreshment and direction for our labor of love. "To him that knoweth to do good, and doeth it not, to him it is sin" (James 4:17). We need to physically come aside periodically and allow the renewing work of God's Spirit to restore our entire being—spirit, soul, and body. Daily times of refreshing are needed. The weekly day of rest was wisely ordered of the Lord. Longer periods are likewise necessary for the kind of recuperation and visitation which the Holy Spirit desires. In the long run, we will not be able to redeem the time as God requires without being obedient to His divine pattern for periods of rest and renewal. The still, small voice is very still and very small; but very significant.

Some by nature are more reflective and are easily drawn into settings which are conducive to meditation. Their problem is not finding the time for quiet repose, but arising to the call of the Beloved when He moves into the rush-a-day world to reach people who desperately need the peace which only His life can bring. The quiet, studious person would also be content to imprison himself in his ivory tower of solitude, not realizing that this is the surest way to convert a reflecting pool into a stagnant pond. We are refreshed and renewed that we might vigorously fulfill our function in the Body of Christ and communicate His life to others.

How the Adversary would dearly love to move us to an extreme position. While we all probably tend toward one pole or the other in a general sense, it is possible to be hyper-active in a specific area of our lives and hypo-active in another. The same might be true as we develop over a period of time. At one phase in our lives we might be a whirlpool of activity until we wear ourselves out, hyper-react, and become a stagnant pond. The Holy Spirit will, however, eventually stabilize our behavior if the basic inclination of our heart is to remain submitted to Him. Each phase of growth brings a better balance to our life and ministry.

The River of Maturity

Having considered the various developmental stages in the life-cycle of our river, we are ready to examine its character as it approaches maturity. Something of each of the preceding phases remains, but there is a depth and breadth in dimension which was not present earlier in its course. There is a powerful sense of direction as it moves purposefully toward the sea. The mighty Columbia which divides the states of Oregon and Washington in its route to the Pacific Ocean is a beautiful example of the mature river. Its potential energy has been usefully harnessed by the Bonneville Dam, where the magnificent falls of water are an evidence of power with purpose. The whole valley is aglow with the electricity produced by its hydroelectric plant. The river's transporting power has carried ships and boats for pleasure and commerce. Vast amounts of timber harvested from the nearby forests have efficiently and effortlessly been floated to the mills on the broad shoulders of old-man river.

Yes, our river has become of age. There is still the rippling laughter of the occasional rapids, but this is interspersed with long stretches of riverside which could be best expressed by a word-picture of peaceful power. Its path is no longer easily deflected by little irregularities in the streambed, but becomes straighter and more direct as the sea is approached. Its race has been won, and soon it will triumphantly merge with the vast waters of its fatherland, the Pacific Ocean.

What a meaningful picture of mature Christian experience! Peace, power, and purpose, all combined into a depth and breadth of character which commands one's respect and appreciation. I have met seasoned saints of God whose lives displayed the maturity we have just described. I am sure the apostle Paul was such a man. It is a noble goal for us all. Each stage in our spiritual development—like our river story—has a necessary place and contribution to make to our life in Christ, but we must not become charmed by any one phase to the point it impedes our further progress. A river flows only in one direction; we cannot recapture the simple character of previous stages. As we move on, however, we shall discover that unique aspects of each phase will remain, balanced and enhanced by each other.

Conclusion

Each of us has been created with a uniqueness in personality. Maturity of expression does not mean conformity without diversity in character. There are many large rivers in the world, but no two of them are exactly alike. We may all pass through similar developmental phases, but each contribution is personally somewhat different, so the mature product is a fulfillment rather than a denial of our distinctive traits.

Our Heavenly Father has always desired a family through which the infinite wonder and beauty of His Son could be expressed. The river of life must flow forever, and must involve all of our unique personalities, for only in this way could the diverse qualities of eternal life be fully expressed. This is the abundant life which is ours in Christ Jesus. It is a life of liberty which begins when our lives are indwelt and filled to overflowing with His Spirit of love. Truly, Christ has SET OUR SPIRITS FREE—now and forever!